Edwin Robert Anderson Seligman

Railway Tariffs and the Interstate Commerce Law

Edwin Robert Anderson Seligman

Railway Tariffs and the Interstate Commerce Law

ISBN/EAN: 9783744662321

Printed in Europe, USA, Canada, Australia, Japan

Cover: Foto ©Suzi / pixelio.de

More available books at **www.hansebooks.com**

RAILWAY TARIFFS

AND THE

INTERSTATE COMMERCE LAW

BY

EDWIN R. A. SELIGMAN, Ph. D.
SCHOOL OF POLITICAL SCIENCE,
COLUMBIA COLLEGE

Reprinted from Political Science Quarterly, Vol. II., Nos. 2 and 3.

GINN & COMPANY
BOSTON, NEW YORK, AND CHICAGO
1887

TABLE OF CONTENTS.

I.

	PAGE
Nature of the railway	1
The principle of tariffs	2
Fixed charges *versus* operating expenses	3
Cost of service theory	4
Charging what the traffic will bear	8
Classification	9
Its legitimacy	11
The abuses	12
Advisory boards	13
Discrimination	14
Personal discrimination	15
Allowance for quantity	16
Wholesale principle	17
Local discrimination	19
Its legitimacy	20
Pro rata charges	21
Value of service principle	23
Not new	23
Analogy to principles of taxation	25
Doctrine of compensation	28
Preferential *versus* differential rates	29
The three forms of differential rates	30
New rates below additional movement expenses	30
Other differential rates	31
Geographical advantages	31
Interests of consumers	32
Distinction between personal and local discriminations	32
The abuses	33
The short haul system	34
Limitations on the principle	35
Short haul laws in the commonwealths	36
Short haul laws in Europe	38

TABLE OF CONTENTS.

	PAGE
The short haul clause in the interstate commerce law	41
Dangers of strict interpretation	42

II.

The anti-pooling clause of the interstate commerce law	43
The doctrine of free competition	43
Economic or industrial monopolies	45
Are combinations an evil?	46
Competition in railways illusory	48
Seven forms of combination	49
Agreement to make equal rates	50
Working arrangement	50
Division of the field or territorialization	50
Division of the traffic	52
Division of the earnings	52
Advantages of pools	
Stability of charges	52
Lessening of personal discriminations	53
Money pools and traffic pools in the United States	55
Net money *versus* gross money pools	56
Pools in Europe	57
England. Joint purse arrangements	57
Germany. Kartellen	59
Austria and Belgium	60
France. Division du traffic	61
Other European countries	61
Dangers of pools	62
Pooling does not prevent healthy competition	63
Abolition of pools would result in final consolidation	63
Differential pools	65
Mistake of the interstate commerce law	65
Senate select committee	67

Competition of carriers on the line	68
History of the system	68
Objections to the project	70

TABLE OF CONTENTS.

	PAGE
Separation of traction and carrier	72
Running powers or compulsory competition	74
Water competition	75
The interstate commerce commission	77
English Commissions	78
Railway commission of 1873	79
Its defects	80
Railway legislation in the United States	81
The granger movement	82
Compulsory commissions	83
Advisory commissions	83
The federal commission	84
Conclusion	85
Good features of the law	85
Error of anti-pooling clause	86
Dangers of the short haul clause	86
Probable results	87

RAILWAY TARIFFS AND THE INTERSTATE COMMERCE LAW.

WHEN Solomon de Cause first advanced the idea of employing steam as a propelling power, in 1615, he was shut up in the mad-house as a hopeless maniac. Two centuries later, in 1812, when Colonel Stevens of Hoboken proposed to build a steam railway at far less cost than the projected Erie canal, he was regarded as absurdly visionary and somewhat demented. And yet to-day, within the short span of a human life, we have the vast network of over three hundred thousand miles of iron roads covering the civilized world. It is the central factor of recent economic development. Little wonder, then, that the weighty problems of railway management in its relations to the owners, the employees, and the public, should engross the earnest attention of legislators and publicists throughout the world.

The Interstate Commerce law of 1887 is the first serious attempt at governmental regulation for the whole of the United States. It may be well, therefore, to discuss the provisions of the act in the light of general principles. We shall confine ourselves primarily to a consideration of the railway tariffs, and attempt to ascertain the underlying doctrines and their limitations.

Railway tariffs may be regarded from two essentially different standpoints, — the private and the public. In so far as a railway is a business corporation, it is a private matter. It may fix its prices in accordance with general business principles. It will endeavor to subserve primarily the interests of its owners. It will strive for the greatest possible profits. Its course is legitimate and praiseworthy. But in so far as the railway forms our public highway, it is a public matter. The objective point now is the general welfare, the interests of the community. It aims not at the greatest possible profits, but at the greatest possible benefits. It looks not at the interests of its owners, but at the interests of the public. The one point of view is individual, the other is social. The modern railway corporation shares both these characteristics. Its nature is hybrid. To subordinate the public to the private element is plainly inadmissible. To entirely engulf the private in the public element is equally unfair, as long as the railway is not owned by the state. Given the private corporation, the question is: How shall the two elements be reconciled? It is the problem of railway legislation and corporate regulation.

The inequality of railroad charges forms the pith of the complaints usually made. It is the crucial point of corporate management. On the one hand we have the anti-monopolists, who liken the common carriers to the feudal barons of old, using the mediæval weapons of unjust privilege and ill-gotten power to carry out their ends of rapacity and favoritism. On the other side we have the railway managers, who exultingly exclaim, in so far as charges are concerned: All that is, is just. Where now is the truth of the matter?

The principle commonly advanced by the antagonists of the railways, as well as by the would-be reformers, is that of cost of service. Charges should be regulated in accordance with the cost of the particular transaction to the company. This is certainly not the actual method. Is it the correct method? Let us see.

Railway expenses are divided into two great classes, — fixed charges and operating expenses. By fixed charges is simply meant the interest account, the sum necessary to meet the periodically recurring interest on the mortgage debt.[1]

---

[1] In Europe, not only the interest on the funded debt, but also the dividends on the capital stock are sometimes included in the "fixed charges." This is manifestly fallacious, as it is not legitimate to class as expenses what are really profits. Rates are nowhere determined by the prospective profits, but *vice versa*. *Cf.* Nördling, Die Selbstkosten des Eisenbahntransports und die Wasserstrassenfrage, (Vienna, 1885,) S. 206–210. The matter is, however, of less importance from the fact that with us railways are generally constructed on the proceeds of the mortgage bonds, not of the capital stock, as in Europe. The interest, hence, far exceeds the dividends. In 1885,

The proportion of fixed charges to operating expenses varies, of course, with each line. A careful calculation on the different branches of a single road found the interest charges to vary from 26 per cent to 59 per cent of the total expenses.[1] But in a rough way it may be said that fixed charges amount to from forty to fifty per cent of the entire expenditures, not alone with us, but also in Europe.[2] In other words, well-nigh half the expenses are constant or invariable. They do not change with the amount of business transacted, but are independent of the traffic. They remain the same whether there be much, little, or no additional traffic.

On the other hand, the operating expenses may be divided into several categories. No uniformity has as yet been attained in the classification of expenses, although the national commission has been empowered to prescribe a uniform system. One method is to divide the expenses into: (*a*) maintenance of road, buildings, and general expenses; (*b*) station expenses; and (*c*) movement expenses. Class *a* will in general be but very slightly affected by the amount of business transacted. Considerable variations in the traffic may take place without a proportionate, if any, increase in the expense involved. They may therefore likewise be set down as constant or invariable expenses. Class *b* will vary, but only in part, with the business transacted. A certain organization must always be maintained, whether the traffic be heavy or light; but after a definite limit is passed, more men must be employed to do more business. These expenses are thus only partially constant. Class *c*, finally, fluctuates almost in proportion to the business transacted. The less trains, the less expense.

The proportion of each of these three classes to the whole will

---

e.g., 186 million dollars were paid in interest, 77 millions in dividends. *Cf.* Poor's Manual for 1886, p. i. For European figures, see Loisel, Annuaire spécial des chemins de fer belges, 1886, pp. 246 *et seq.*

[1] Fink, Cost of Railroad Transportation (1882), table A, p. 4, for the Louisville and Nashville Railroad.

[2] See the tables in Sax, Die Verkehrsmittel in Stats- und Volkswirthschaft, (1879), Bd. II, S. 368. For France in particular, Baum, Annales des ponts et chaussées, Mémoires, 5me série, t. i, p. 422,

of course vary with the widely different characteristics of each line; but in general it may be affirmed that about one-half of the operating expenses are constant or invariable.[1]

The total constant expenditures of a railway are thus the fixed charges plus one-half the operating expenses. In other words, a large majority of railway expenses are irrespective of the amount of business. They remain the same, notwithstanding an increase or decrease of the traffic.

This distinction between constant and fluctuating expenses is of vital importance to a correct understanding of the principle of railway rates. It leads to certain conclusions which form the fundamental explanations of actual tariffs.

It is unnecessary to explain the wide disparity of cost of carriage on different lines, or for individual transactions. Certain characteristics affect the roads themselves, such as the grades, the curves, the weight, and speed of the trains, the cost of construction, the quality of the supplies, the changing conditions under which the service is performed at different seasons, *etc*. These alone would show how difficult is the task of accurately determining the cost of carriage for any one service. But the task is complicated by other difficulties. It is apparent that the cost of transportation per ton-mile must vary with the tons and the miles, *i.e.*, with the quantity of the freight and the length of the haul. But these differ widely in each case. On one line the greater portion of the freight is carried over its whole length; on another the local business far outweighs the through

---

[1] Manager Haines, of the Savan. Fla. & W. R. R., divides operating expenses into five classes, and makes a careful calculation that 53 per cent of such expenses do not increase with additional business. Report of Senate Select Committee on Interstate Commerce (1886), App., p. 138. We shall hereafter speak of this as the Cullom report.

[2] Mr. Fink's calculation varies but slightly from the above. He asserts that upon an average of $1 earned in the roads of the United States, 40 cents are required to pay 4½ per cent interest on bonds and stock, 35 cents to pay the movement expenses, and 25 cents to pay maintenance and general expenses. Cullom Committee, Test., p. 95. The New York commission divide operating expenses into maintenance, general and transportation (including station) expenses. But the result is the same. For Europe, see Ulrich, Das Eisenbahn-Tarifwesen (1886), S. 40, but corrected as to Germany in Archiv für Eisenbahnwesen, 1887, S. 253.

traffic, so that the capacity of the rolling stock is not fully utilized. On one line the traffic moves in great part in one direction, and the number of empty cars returned is abnormally large; on another there is far more back-loading and a more even distribution of the traffic. On one line the trains are started with full loads, on another they are half empty. The proportion of paying to dead weight, or the amount of the tare, is of paramount importance.[1] All these causes influence both the tons and the miles, and thus affect the cost per ton-mile.

Logically, the cost per ton-mile is resolvable into two portions, — that which corresponds to the constant or fixed expenses, and that which corresponds to the fluctuating or variable expenses. The former portion is ascertained simply by dividing the constant expenses by the total ton-miles. It will therefore vary inversely to the traffic.[2] But as the constant expenses form by far the larger portion of the whole, the rate per ton-mile will be determined by this corresponding portion. We conclude then that the cost tends to vary almost inversely to the traffic — the more traffic, the less the cost per ton-mile; the less traffic, the greater the cost per ton-mile. That is to say, even if it were feasible to construct a tariff based on the cost of service of each particular transaction, — in itself a work of gigantic magnitude and infinite difficulty, — such a tariff would be of very slight avail unless the amount of freight remained an unalterable quantity. So soon as the volume of traffic changes, the cost of service is necessarily altered. The rate would no longer be based on cost of service.

---

[1] The *average* gross weight of freight cars of all classes in the United States is eight tons per car. The average load they carry is five tons. Hence, 59 per cent of the weight hauled in freight traffic is non-paying or dead weight. In passenger traffic the non-paying load is almost 90 per cent, because the cars are not so fully packed. In Germany, in 1880, the dead weight was: for freight cars, 53 per cent (or taking only the loaded cars, 27 per cent); for passenger cars, 76 per cent; for baggage cars, 97 per cent.

[2] Suppose the constant expenditures for transporting seven and a half million ton-miles amount to $75,000. Then —

if there are 7,500,000 ton-miles, cost $= \frac{75,000}{7,500,000} = 1$ c. per ton-mile;
if there are 10,000,000 ton-miles, cost $= \frac{75,000}{10,000,000} = 0.75$ c. per ton-mile;
if there are 5,000,000 ton-miles, cost $= \frac{75,000}{5,000,000} = 1.5$ c. per ton-mile.

Furthermore, the amount of traffic itself depends to a large extent on the rate. Low rates produce large traffic, high rates make little traffic. This has led to the paradoxical conclusion that cost of service depends on the rate, and not inversely that the rate depends on cost of service. We thus have a curious interaction of cause and effect. But of course this is true only within certain limits, and subject to serious qualifications. The success of a decrease of rates in attracting additional business will operate only up to that point where increased traffic does not imply disproportionately increased expenses. If the additional business necessitates large expenses, like a double track, it may cost more than it is worth. Low rates do not always increase net profits. Again, the success of a decrease of rates will diminish with every successive diminution of the rates. There is a certain limit beyond which the efficacy of reduced rates as a financial venture becomes very problematical. The business is not expansible. On this account the railways rarely reduce charges simultaneously on all kinds of traffic, but experiment gradually with special classes or kinds of business, and even then are often unwilling to undertake the reduction at all.[1]

But if it is even partially true that cost of service depends on the traffic, and therefore on the rate, it cannot be wholly true that the rate depends on the cost of service. The two principles are mutually contradictory. We are thus logically forced to the conclusion that railway charges are not and cannot be based on cost of service alone.

Cost of service does not fix rates. It forms in the long run only the minimum limit of rates. A well-managed road will not consciously continue a losing business, unless, indeed, it be

---

[1] In regard to freight traffic, the above statement is notoriously true. In regard to passenger traffic, *cf.* the history of third-class traffic in England. In 1844 the railways had to be compelled by law to run cheap trains for third-class passengers, their opposition being silenced only by exempting these trains from the passenger duties. But before long these very trains resulted in immense profits, and to-day constitute by far the most lucrative portion of the passenger business. *Cf.* also the strenuous opposition of the New York elevated railroad to the five-cent bill, while to-day the profits are immensely increased by the voluntary reduction.

operated by the state as a tax on the community, and no serious thinker has yet proposed this method of running railways. Differences in cost of service between two roads result not in proportionate differences in rates, but simply in different profits. Differences in cost cannot imply corresponding differences of rates. The principle is as applicable to portions of the same line as to different lines, since no two parts of the same line have the same cost of service, and hence if the principle were consistently applied, it would be necessary to make a different rate for each mile of every road, which is absurd. But if rates are fixed according to the *average* cost of service for the whole line, they may equally well be fixed for the average cost of services on all business, in which cases the element of difference of cost for each particular transaction is entirely eliminated. No freight is ever shipped at the average cost of service.

It would hence be foreign to our purpose to attempt an exact mathematical computation of the cost of service. Not only would it be necessary to ascertain the exact percentage of fixed to variable expenses in each particular case, but further to calculate the exact proportion of increase of cost to increase of traffic. Numerous endeavors have been made, but no two agree.[1] And even if successful they would, as we see, be of very slight practical utility.

The cost of service principle is neither practised nor practicable. The attempt to base rates solely in cost is a pure chimera. Well-nigh every expert, whether scientist,[2] official, or legislator, and every parliamentary commission, from the early English to the late Italian and American, absolutely discards it as a principle.[3] But although the rule is impracticable, it is

---

[1] *Cf.* the works of Chanute, Morehouse, Fink, Kirkman, in America; of Fairbairn, Gordon, Lardner, in England; of Garke, Scheffler, Schüller, Schübler, Nördling, in Germany; of Baum, Jacqmin, Gournerie, Brière, in France; of Brioschi, Genala, Calvori, in Italy.

[2] Even Wagner, the great apostle of state railways, comes to the same conclusion in his last edition. Finanzwissenschaft, 3. Ausg., I, 760–763.

[3] "The movement of a commodity by rail is determined by considerations wholly independent of and not affected by the cost of the service to be performed." Cullom Com. Rep., p. 184. For Italy, *cf.* Atti della Commissione d' Inchiesta sull' esercizio

asserted by some to be the only just, the ideal method. Before discussing this, let us ascertain the actual principle according to which tariffs are arranged. Only then shall we be able to answer the question of the relative justifiability of the two principles.

How, then, are rates actually fixed? The object of a railway is to make the greatest possible net profits, *i.e.*, to increase its traffic and to decrease its expenses. This it finds can be best attained by lowering the charges on certain classes of goods, or on the same classes to different localities. In other words, what decides the manager is not so much the *cost* of the service as the *value* of the service. This practice has been called "charging what the traffic will bear," an unfortunate expression and liable to much misconception. Charging what the traffic will bear, correctly understood, simply serves as an excuse for reducing rates on the low-class traffic, because it cannot bear higher rates. The phrase is a bad one, because it may be interpreted into meaning that the greatest possible charges on high-class goods are also legitimate. Correctly understood, it justifies lower charges on certain kinds of business; incorrectly understood, it seems to justify extortionate charges on other kinds of business.[1]

Charging what the traffic will bear, in its strict sense, does not fix rates; it determines only the maximum limit of charges, just as mere cost of hauling fixes the minimum limit. Between these limits the rate varies with the value of the service, or, as is sometimes said, is made to conform to the requirements of trade. It becomes a commercial question, and subject to the law of supply and demand. In so far it is a purely private

delle ferrovie italiane (1881), Parte II, Riassunto, II, 932–953. For England, *cf.* Joint Select Committee on Railway Cos. Amalgamation (1872), pp. xxxiii and li. For France, see Rapport de Waddington (1880), in Picard, Chemins de fer français, t. 5 (1884), p. 128. *Cf.* also the statement of the advisory commission on differential rates to the seaboard (Thurman, Washburne, and Cooley) in Proceedings of the Joint Executive Committee (1882), p. 29.

[1] The celebrated phrase of M. Solacroup, the French railway director, is hence regrettable: "En matière de tarification de transports il n'y a qu'une seule règle qui soit rationnelle; c'est de demander à la marchandise tout ce qu'elle peut payer. Tout autre principe est arbitraire." Professor Villey calls it "une phrase vide de sens." Traité d'économie politique (1885), p. 206.

matter. But the railway is also partly a public institution : hence the necessity for important qualifications of the private business principle, for serious limitations of the law of supply and demand. These qualifications and these limitations have often been completely ignored by the railways, because of their mistaken assumption of being purely private enterprises. Let us study the limitations as well as the principle.

Charging according to what the service is worth results in the two fundamental principles of classification and discrimination.[1] Classification is due to the fact that the same service has a varying value when rendered to different commodities. Discrimination (*i.e.*, local discrimination) is due to the fact that the same service has a varying value when rendered to different places. Whether the same service has a varying value for the freight of different persons, and may thus give rise to personal discriminations, is a question to be treated by itself.

Classification. Value of service influences classification in a double way: it puts the same articles into different classes ; it puts different articles into different classes. It puts the same articles into different classes according to the methods of transportation, and makes a distinction between slow and fast delivery. With us this takes the form of freight and express traffic. Our general classification applies only to freight traffic. In Europe, where separate express companies are unknown, the rates are graduated according to this distinction — goods and parcels rates, *petite* and *grande vitesse*, *Frachtgut* and *Eilgut*. Such a classification is of course perfectly legitimate, whether from the standpoint of value or from that of cost of service. The better service benefits the goods and increases the expenses of the railway.

---

[1] The word discrimination is not always used in the same sense. Some use it to imply any variation from the cost of service, and make it include classification, which is to them a discrimination between articles as opposed to a discrimination between persons or places. But this is misleading. A classification as between two articles may be due to a difference in cost of service, in which case there would be no discrimination in the above sense. To make classification of this kind a part of discrimination is illogical. It is far preferable to separate the two terms completely, defining discrimination as is done on page 236.

Far more important, however, is the classification of different articles into different categories. The primary element here again is value of service. Cost of service, indeed, influences classification to a minor extent in so far as the articles differ in bulk, shape, risk, direction, or regularity of shipment. By bulk is meant the proportion of dead to paying weight. One car may be filled with 2000 lbs. of baskets, another with 30,000 lbs. of iron or sand, and yet the cost of moving the cars may not appreciably differ. Manifestly, the charge per 100 lbs. on baskets should be higher than on iron or sand. The tare becomes an important factor of the cost. Actual computations again have demonstrated that the shape of the articles influences the cost, especially the terminal expenses, far more than might at first appear. The risk, when incurred by the railway, is also a legitimate ingredient of cost, and varies greatly with the nature of the article. The question of direction involves that of back-loading and affects articles differently on each particular line. Finally, some articles are sent intermittently in small lots, while others are shipped with great regularity and in such quantities that the railway can easily accommodate itself to the traffic. Every shipment has its own peculiarities, and it thus happens that articles of equal value may be put into different classes.

But actual rates are mainly fixed not by cost of service, but by what the service is worth. Classification depends only in a subordinate degree upon cost. The controlling element is value, not cost. Cheap goods must be charged less than dear goods although the cost of service may be greater. The main point is the development of the traffic. The goods must not be charged so high rates as to render their transportation impossible or unprofitable. We must keep in mind the distinction between the fixed and the variable expenses. If the freight can be secured at rates which will more than cover the variable expenses,—the actual hauling and a proportionate part of the station expenses,—it will pay the road to take this freight, because an addition, however small, is thereby made to the fixed expenses. These would have to be met at all events, whether that particular freight were taken or not. A small contribution to fixed expenses is better than none at all. The choice is between freight at a rate slightly above mere cost of operation, and no freight. Yet to apply this low rate to all commodities would of course render it impossible to meet the fixed expenses or earn profits. In other words, it is profitable for a railway to transport certain classes of freight at rates which if extended to all business would ruin the company. Classification of freight is not only necessary, but justifiable and beneficial. The meagre surplus over hauling expenses in the cheap goods contributes, if ever so little, to the fixed expenses, and diminishes to this extent the amount which it is necessary to raise from the remaining traffic. The higher-class goods can be transported at rates which are lower than would otherwise be the case. If we had no classification, not only would we not have cheap wheat or cheap meat, but the charges on all the other articles would be raised per ton-mile. It reduces the rates on the cheap goods immensely, and the rate on the dear goods moderately. Classification is based, in the main, on the principle of value of service. An advance of ten cents per hundred pounds on coal would soon make its influence felt, and might double or treble its value; a similar advance on silks or dry goods would exert but an inappreciable influence on their value.[1] The same rate which would prohibit the transportation of one commodity may scarcely be felt by another. The principle of classification is the first corollary from the distinction between fixed and variable expenditures.

To uphold the legitimacy and necessity of classification is, however, quite another thing from maintaining the justifiability of all actual tariffs or from attempting to palliate undeniable abuses. The early roads started with but little classification. The first English charters indeed contained statutory maxima for a number of articles. The Stockton and Darlington Railway act prescribed three classes, the Liverpool and Manchester

[1] Articles are thus classified primarily and chiefly according to their value; but the classification is modified by the tare, *i.e.*, proportion of dead to paying weight, and in exceptional instances by the other considerations of cost.

act five classes.[1] These were based chiefly on the old canal acts. In the United States very few of the state charters fixed either maxima or classification.[2] The result was a very simple system. It was found, however, that a gradual modification and differentiation of the charges conduced not only to a development of the traffic, but also to a growth of business prosperity. But the matter of classification with us to-day is in a well-nigh chaotic state. It is made to depend on the numberless exigencies and conditions of business life. It is lacking in uniformity, in stability, and very often in justice. The tariffs of the present day on our main lines are a great advance upon those of several years ago, but there is still enormous ground for improvement. The point to be noticed is that these wide powers of fixing the classes are put in the hands of private individuals as sole arbiters. While the principle of classification is perfectly just, the liability to abuse of the principle arises from the fact that the authority is given to only one of the parties in interest. It is this which arouses the indignation of the public and emphasizes the necessity of public control.

But we must be careful not to let our indignation carry us too far. The abuses of classification are on the whole the lesser abuses of railway management. They take place only within narrow limits, because it is the interest of the railway manager to charge those rates which tend to develop the traffic. Exorbitant charges for any class will lead to decreased shipments. Mistakes may be made, but when the railway is honestly managed the mistakes will be rectified. The great advantage of the traffic associations or pools is that they minimize the danger of dishonest management in any single road, and bring about a greater uniformity and stability. The dressed-beef controversy is a case in point.[3] We do not

---

[1] Some of the earliest toll and maximum rate clauses are reprinted in Grierson, Railway Rates (1886), pp. lxv–lxxii. Also, more fully, in Report of Select Committee on Railways (1881), part ii, app. no. 55.

[2] For a good collection of the earliest charters, see G^{me} Tell Poussin, Chemins de fer américains (1836), pp. 211–271. See also W. P. Gregg and B. Pond, The Railroad Laws and Charters of the United States. (Boston, 1851.)

[3] See Proceedings and Circulars of the Joint Executive Committee, Freight De-

imply, with many of our eloquent railway officials, that there is a necessary identity of interests between the railways and the people. Our past history unfortunately does not bear this out. It would be absurd to depend on this imagined harmony as a remedy for actual abuses. But it is equally foolish to go to the other extreme with popular demagogues. Classification should indeed be supervised by public authorities, but the demand for a rigid law prescribing all details, would impute to our legislators a knowledge which they cannot possess. And those who advocate state management in the United States forget to think of the havoc that would be created by the simple political influence of our law-makers. A congressman represents a district noted for the production or manufacture of certain articles; what more simple method of appeasing the clamor of his constituents than by changing the article in question from class 3 to class 4? Were the state to own the railways under our actual political system, the claims upon our legislators for spoils would be increased a thousand-fold. To cure the abuses of classification by letting our congressmen fix the classification would indeed be jumping from the frying-pan into the fire.

An escape from the dilemma seems to be outlined in the principle of advisory boards or consultative councils akin to those lately instituted in Europe. The German local councils[1] are elected by the chambers of commerce and agriculture, and it is incumbent on the railway officials to consult with them on all important questions affecting the tariffs. True, the decision lies ultimately in the hands of the railway authorities, but these are public, administrative officials. The system has worked admirably. In Italy, where the law of 1885 has prescribed eight uniform classes for all the lines, a council with subordinate divisions composed of railway and state officials as well as representatives of commercial interests

---

partment, for 1884, (N. Y. 1885,) pp. 90–95, 161, *etc*. *Cf*. also the recent unification of east and west bound trunk-line tariffs to six classes, in place of four and thirteen.

[1] Bezirks-Eisenbahnräthe.

supervise the actual charges.[1] In France, where nothing similar exists, notwithstanding the ministerial *homologation* or approval of rates, the state is still struggling with the railways in the endeavor to bring about a simplified classification. England's condition is almost as chaotic as ours.[2] Of the attempt to suppress all abuses of classification by the heroic step of abolishing or restricting classification itself, as in the compromise or car-space system of central Europe, we shall have more to say later on. Classification *per se* is legitimate.

As opposed to classification a *discrimination* may be defined as an inequality in the charge for hauling a like quantity of similar articles for an equal distance in the same manner. The definition includes four points. The quantity, the articles, the distance, and the manner of transportation must be the same.[3] If a railway charges in one case one cent per ton-mile for wood between Hartford and New York, and in another case two cents, this is a discrimination. It may take place because two different persons sent it from Hartford or because in the one case the wood was shipped at Hartford and in the other at Boston. All discrimination is hence either personal or local. A personal discrimination is called a preferential rate; a local discrimination is called a differential rate.[4] Let us analyze each.

---

[1] Consiglio per l' esame delle tariffe ferroviarie.

[2] Lord Stanley's bill of 1887, § 24, like Mundella's bill of 1886, provides for a revision of the classification by the Board of Trade, to be ultimately enforced by law. This is a step in advance, — perhaps too great a step.

[3] To haul one ton for 2 cents and two tons for 4 cents; to haul coal for 2 cents and wood for 4 cents; to haul coal one mile for 2 cents and two miles for 4 cents; to haul wood for 2 cents by slow freight and for 4 cents by fast freight or express, is thus no discrimination. In each case one of the four elements of the definition is lacking.

Hadley, Railroad Transportation (1885), p. 108, defines discrimination as a difference in rates not based on corresponding difference in cost. This is manifestly incorrect. The cost of service per ton-mile from A to B may be $1\frac{1}{4}$ cents, from A to C, a station further on, only 1 cent (since cost decreases with distance). This difference in charges to B and C is a discrimination against B, although based on a corresponding difference in cost. It may be a valid discrimination, but it is a discrimination, and is everywhere regarded as such. The same holds true of personal discriminations, which may sometimes be proportional to cost of service. Then, again, Professor Hadley makes discrimination include classification. But, as we have seen, classification may be partly based on cost of service.

[4] This nomenclature, although exact, is not always followed. It is used in the

Personal discrimination. Differences in rates based on classification we found to be essentially legitimate. It is difficult, however, to find any principle on which to base distinctions between two or more shippers for a similar service. Personal discriminations are beyond cavil the most flagitious abuses of arbitrary railway management. Concessions made to large shippers do not, up to a certain point, come within this general condemnation. Allowance for quantity or making a distinction, *e.g.*, between car-loads and less than car-loads is within certain limits defensible, and is practised in some shape in every country. But this is really a matter of classification, and may be upheld by the advocates of cost of service in the same way that classification into slow freight and express is defended. A well-filled car costs undeniably less in proportion than a half-filled car. But the difficulty is to select the unit of classification above which the rates shall be the same for all persons. Shall it be the pound, hundredweight, ton, or car-load; or shall there be no unit at all? No country has as yet adopted the pound as a unit. In England we have the "smalls" carried at lower rates, and other distinctions made in the mineral and special classes. With us the common unit is the hundredweight, because of the diversity of our car-loads, which vary from 20,000 to 60,000 lbs. The classification, however, generally specifies the minimum weight which entitles to car-load rates. Distinctions between ordinary and car-loads are everywhere permitted, and one of the fundamental principles of the "natural" and "reform" tariffs in Germany is that rates should differ with the quantities of freight (up to ten tons). Of course it costs

---

English Select Com. (1881) Evid. qu. 13302. Some make "differential" rates cover all discriminations, so that a preferential rate would be a differential rate. Others again call all discriminations preferential rates. But this is confusing. In the United States "differential" rate is sometimes used in a peculiar sense. The rate from Chicago to New York, *e.g.*, is taken as a basis. A certain number of cents are added to or subtracted from this rate for all stations west or east of Chicago. These variations are termed *differentials* and are based to some extent on distance. The effect of these "differentials" is thus to attain an approximate equality of charge per ton-mile, while a differential rate as commonly understood in European practice and in scientific works all over the world amounts simply to a discriminating rate or an absence of equality of charge. The latter method is more logical and scientific.

less to transport car-loads than single lots, but that is due only to the amount of the tare. If the single lots are packed closely, so as to fill the car, their dead weight would be greatly diminished. At all events it is almost impossible to fix the exact difference of cost, and in very few instances do the differences in cost warrant the actual discriminations.[1] So that, even if we adopt the principle of cost of service, the distinction between car-loads and smaller shipments is only partially justifiable and may often work injustice to the small shipper. The attempt, however, to make the pound the unit of shipment would still be premature, although it may be the ultimate outcome of the controversy. Allowance for quantity below a moderate limit excites but little complaint and increases the efficiency of the railway.

But if this comparatively unimportant difference — which is in reality a species of classification — be in itself only partially justifiable, what shall we say of those vastly greater discriminations which cannot even claim cost of service as an ostensible reason? Such a practice is indefensible on any theory whatsoever. To build up one man's business at the expense of another can never be acknowledged a legitimate function of the common carriers. To give this power to private corporations would be to strike at the root of commercial prosperity. Such discriminations are sometimes defended on the plea of allowance for quantity. But allowance for quantity not based on cost of service is robbed of all pretext for existence. Whether a train-load is hauled for one shipper to one consignee, or for ten shippers to ten consignees at the same point makes very little difference in expense to the carrier. Furthermore, the matter rarely arises in this way. In almost every case of concessions to large shippers but few cars are in fact forwarded at a time. The favored shipper's freight is hauled in the same manner as that of his competitors, and the special rates are granted only because of the contract to forward a larger number of cars per

---

[1] See a typical case of rates on base-ball bats to Council Bluffs, where the difference between ordinary and car-load rates amounted to 157 per cent, thus crowding out the small shippers. Cullom Committee Report, Test. (Wicker), p. 759.

month or year.[1] The cost to the railway is not appreciably smaller, but the advantage to the large shipper is obvious. The special rates enable him to control the market, the control of the market secures him the special rates. It is a see-saw working both ways. Allowance for quantity of this kind can hence not be justified even in the partial way that the distinction between car-loads and ordinary freight can be upheld. The cost of service principle cannot be invoked.

Reduced to this extremity, the advocates of personal discrimination are wont to assert that a business firm makes wholesale rates less than retail and gives special figures perhaps to every customer. Why is not the same principle, they ask, applicable to the railroad business? They utterly fail to perceive that a railway is not simply a business corporation, but something far more; that it is a public trust and forms to-day our public highway; that a merchant is not bound to treat his customers equally and may favor his friends without violating any law of business ethics, but that a railway is a body of delegated powers; that it exercises public functions, is invested with public rights, and therefore has public duties. This is the important qualification of the principle that the question of railway rates is a mere commercial question. To make concessions for large shipments is to arrogate powers of wide-reaching potency; it is a claim which cannot be acquiesced in or defended. The wholesale principle or allowance for quantity when carried to this extreme becomes utterly untenable.[2] And

---

[1] Cullom Committee Report, p. 191.

[2] The report of the Hepburn committee is thus open to question: "The principle of wholesale rates enters as legitimately into railroad carriage as into any private business." But this is qualified by the clause: "Where additional quantity ceases to lessen cost of carriage, or be of pecuniary advantage to the road, the differences should cease." Report, p. 65.

An interesting discussion of the principle of wholesale rates as applied to jobbers and retailers may be found in the report of the Iowa commissioners, an exceedingly able body. The celebrated case is Merrill & Keeney *vs.* Chic. & N. W. &c. See Report, 1883, pp. 678–686, and further discussion in Report, 1884, pp. 71–77. The commissioners go too far in the defence of the wholesale principle and err in making classification and differential rates depend upon this principle. They depend on the contrary on the distinction between fixed and variable expenses. Only in so far as allowance for quantity depends on cost of service, is it legitimate. The wholesale

the claim is in fact no longer upheld by our best railroad men.[1] But although no longer theoretically defended, such discriminations are still actually practised. Not only concessions to large shippers, but what is worse, personal discriminations resting on no other basis but pure favoritism, are yet of common occurrence. The revelations of the New York assembly investigation of 1879 are fresh in the minds of all. A great improvement has indeed taken place in the eastern lines, but secret rebates or substantially similar favors are by no means a thing of the past.[2]

Personal discriminations then cannot be defended upon any theory of railway rates. They must be stopped at all hazards. But how? The common law forbids them, but the inhibition of the common law has been of little efficacy. The fear of incurring the displeasure of the railways has acted as a serious check to the institution of suits. To rely on free competition as a panacea is absurd. Personal discriminations are most glaring when competition is most active. Cut-rates and rebates are never so common as during the railway wars. The surest method of preventing personal discriminations is just the opposite, *i.e.*, universal combination or monopoly, in other words state ownership. This in fact was one great reason why the

---

principle *per se* is not applicable to railroads. *Cf.* Test. of Manager Haines, Cullom Com. Rep., App. p. 143. Notwithstanding the report of the Iowa board, the distinction between jobbers and retailers was abandoned. Of late there has been a movement to abolish even car-load rates. But the arguments of the board have thus far prevented it. Report, 1885, pp. 45–53; 1886, pp. 31–46. From the railway standpoint the wholesale principle is indeed a "fundamental truth," as the commission says; but from the public standpoint the "fundamental truth" vanishes. Railway profits, as we shall see, are no excuse for inequality of charge.

[1] *Cf.* Fink in Hepburn Com. Rep. Exhibits, p. 149, and The Railroad Problem and its Solution (1883), pp. 10, 41. — *Cf.* Cullom Com. Rep., Test. of Blanchard, p. 159; Firth, p. 466; Furber, p. 333; Kimball, p. 1238; Mink, p. 437, Wistar, p. 516. [The only two exceptions are Ackerman, p. 604, and Meek, p. 1049.] Also Jewett and Vanderbilt in Hepburn Com. Rep., Test., pp. 1481 and 130. So Alexander, Railway Practice (1887) pp. 21, 59.

[2] *Cf.* the testimony of a railway official: "I have been doing it myself for years, and had to do it." Referring to the effort to get the business of a number of millers from another company, he adds: "I can accomplish my purpose better by picking out one good, smart, live man and giving him a concession; . . . let him go there and scoop the business. I get the tonnage, and that is what I want. . . . You can take hold of one man and build him up at the expense of the others, and the railway will get the tonnage." Cullom Rep., Test. (Wicker), p. 778.

railways were bought up by the Prussian government.[1] But state ownership is out of the question at present in the United States. With our actual political conditions and our unreformed civil service, the abuses would be intensified, not lessened. There are only three methods, or combinations of methods, which can settle the question, — judicial regulation, legislative and administrative regulation, development of the pooling policy. The history and merits of each, as well as the method pursued in the Interstate Commerce law, may be left to the following essay. But preferential rates cannot in any sense be upheld as a corollary of the principle of value.

Local discrimination. Quite different from preferential rates are differential rates. Differential rates may arise in two ways: through the desire of the railway to develop its traffic, or through the action of competitive centres. The road may wish to extend its traffic in commodities coming from a distance. If they are to be carried at all, they must be transported at less than the regular rates. A commodity which comes from a point a thousand miles distant cannot afford to pay the same rate per mile as one which comes ten miles. The traffic will not bear it. To charge the same rate per mile from Kansas to New York as from New Jersey to New York would simply put a stop to the Kansas traffic. Hence arises the necessity of a distinction between local and through rates. Goods coming from a distance must be treated in the same manner as cheap goods. Local discrimination is like classification. The distant freight is the cheap freight, the near freight is the dear freight. The underlying principle again is value of service. The act of transportation adds far more to the value of the distant than to that of the near freight. Annihilation of distance is proportionate increase of value.

But secondly, local discriminations may arise from competition in the centres of traffic, whether the competition be due to railways or waterways. Two lines meet, *e.g.*, in Buffalo. The old line wishes to retain its business, the new line wishes to

---

[1] *Cf.* the argument for state railroad ownership (a translation of a Prussian parliamentary document of 1879), New York, 1880, pp. 43 *et seq.*

develop a new business. Rates from Buffalo to New York will immediately fall, and the competition may be carried so far as to reduce rates to or below the level of mere transportation expenses. Local rates may remain unaffected. The result will be a disproportionately small charge to the point of competition. The number of competitive centres in the United States is immense,[1] the quantity of local discriminations is hence correspondingly large. A lower rate to the competitive centre is the sole condition of the retention of the competitive traffic. Increase of charges means a destruction of the business.[2]

From the standpoint of the railway, therefore, the principle of differential rates is beneficial. It is due in the last instance to the distinction between fixed and variable expenses. Any rate on the through business above mere operating expenses is *pro tanto* profitable. The surplus goes to defray the fixed expenses. Rather than not get the traffic at all, the railway will take it at reduced rates, and yet these reduced rates if applied to all business would be ruinously unprofitable. The charge per mile on the longer haul may be less than the charge per mile on the shorter haul. How much less it may be is of no concern to the railway, as long as operating expenses are paid. The only endeavor is to retain and extend the traffic.

From the standpoint of the public the principle of differential rates is also justifiable — as a principle. The element of competition would in itself not be a valid justification. Whether the freight is carried by one route or another, *ceteris paribus*, makes no difference to the shipper, except indeed that public interest might oppose competition of foreign railways. But the long-haul consideration is of vital importance to the public. It becomes the question of having the goods transported at the lower rates, or not having them transported at all. The industrial progress of the nineteenth century is due to cheapened methods of production. Whatever tends to reduce

[1] In 1886, of the 33,694 railway stations in the United States, 2778 were junction points. Chief of Bureau of Statistics quoted in Congressional Record, Jan. 12, 1887, p. 562.

[2] *Cf.* Michaelis, Die Differentialtarife der Eisenbahnen, Bd. I. (1873); Boinvilliers, Des transports à prix réduits sur les chemins de fer (1878).

the cost of transportation and to eliminate the element of distance in so far increases national prosperity. [Only under a system of differential rates does this development become possible. Without local discriminations the growth of our country would be set back many decades. They form an indispensable condition of national prosperity.]

The legitimacy of the principle of differential rates may be inferred from considering the effects of their abolition. The opposite of a differential rate, *i.e.*, a different charge per mile, is an equal mileage or *pro rata* rate, *i.e.*, the same charge per mile. We pass over the absurd inconsistency of those who in the same breath advocate cost of service and *pro rata* charges. One of the plainest principles of railway economics is that cost of service becomes relatively less as the distance traversed becomes greater. To transport an article twenty miles does not cost twice as much as to transport it ten miles. Only a portion of the expense increases with the distance. The greater part is independent of distance, so that the cost of service diminishes with every additional mile. The separation of terminal charges, which are of course utterly irrespective of the distance traversed, from pure hauling expenses, would diminish, but by no means remove the objection. Hence to base equal mileage rates on the principle of cost of service is illogical. Even according to the doctrine of cost, differential rates are perfectly legitimate. Rates absolutely proportional to cost of service would be differential rates.[1]

But omitting the question of logic, what would be the effect of *pro rata* charges? Here both theory and practice come to our aid. The theoretical conclusions have been well formulated in various governmental commissions, the practical illustrations have been afforded by the working of our Granger laws and, in a greatly modified extent, by the experience of some European railways. Nowhere, perhaps, has the matter been more tersely put than by the English parliamentary committee of 1872:[2]

---

[1] This has led to the sliding scale and zone systems — mileage rates decreasing with distance — in various parts of Europe, and even in the United States.

[2] Joint Select Committee on Railway Cos. Amalgamation, 1872, Rep., p. xxxii,

(*a*) It would prevent railway companies from lowering their fares and rates, so as to compete with traffic by sea, by canal, or by a shorter or otherwise cheaper railway, and would thus deprive the public of the benefit of competition, and the company of a legitimate source of profit.

(*b*) It would prevent railway companies from making perfectly fair arrangements for carrying at a lower rate than usual goods brought in larger and constant quantities, or for carrying for long distances at a lower rate than for short distances.

(*c*) It would compel a company to carry for the same rate over a line which has been very expensive in construction, or which, from gradients or otherwise, is very expensive in working, at the same rate at which it carries over less expensive lines.

In short, to impose equal mileage on the companies would be to deprive the public of the benefit of much of the competition which now exists or has existed, to raise the charges on the public in many cases where the companies now find it to their interest to lower them, and to perpetuate monopolies in carriage, trade, and manufactures, in favor of those rates and places which are nearest or least expensive, where the varying charges of the companies now create competition.

In like manner, the New York commission concludes, after a comprehensive review of the whole subject, that *pro rata* charges are absolutely injudicious and impracticable.[1] The Senate committee of 1886 does not even consider the proposition worth a separate discussion. The late French and Italian commissions hold the same views.[2] American experience is no less emphatic. The first Granger law, enacted in Michigan in 1871, prescribed equal mileage rates — with a slight modification for short distances. Even as changed by the law of 1873 these rates were so utterly impracticable that they were disregarded by the railways with the tacit consent of the people. The com-

where the conclusions of the Royal Commissions of 1865 are simply re-formulated. The Select Committee of 1882 reprints the conclusions and discusses them at length. Report, pp. ix *et seq.*

[1] Report of the Board of Railroad Commissioners on the *pro rata* bill (1884), p. 125. Also the annual report for 1884, App. 63. *Pro rata* laws are described as "straight-jackets, preventing perhaps some positive evil, but dulling the energy and cramping the development of business. They hamper legitimate efforts at expansion."

[2] "È altresi un fatto incontestabile che il sistema delle tariffe differenziali ha contribuito a rendere più forti e migliori le industrie nazionali," *etc.* Atti della Commissione d'Inchiesta (1881), Riassunto, II, 832. For France see the report translated in the English Select Com. Rep. (1882), App., especially p. 450.

missioner pronounced the duties imposed upon him impossible of accomplishment.[1] The fixed-distance tariff of Iowa, according to the law of 1874, proved to be so unequal and unjust in its operation that it was repealed shortly after.[2] The results of the Potter law of 1874, in Wisconsin, and of similar enactments in Minnesota and Illinois, were equally convincing. They proved to be rather a burden than a relief. The demand for equal mileage rates is an emanation of crude ideas; the outcome of a laudable demand for equality, which would in actual practice result in glaring inequality and in an abandonment of the greatest benefits conferred by railroad transportation. Differential rates or local discriminations form a necessary part of all railway management.[3] They constitute the second corollary from the distinction between fixed and variable expenditures.

The principle of value of service may thus be analyzed into the two constituent elements of classification and local discrimination. But now the question arises: Is value of service indeed a just basis for railway charges? Should not cost of service be preferred? We leave the domain of practicability and come to the field of justice.

Let us first ascertain whether the value-of-service principle is indeed so novel in transportation charges as the anti-monopoly league and others maintain. This assertion may be categorically denied. The old turnpike tolls in England, as in America, whether for vehicles or animals, were not the same for all, but were divided into different categories. The English turnpike acts fixed higher rates for coaches than for dray wagons; according to the doctrinc of cost of service they should have done the opposite. In France the charges on the highways varied not only from road to road, but frequently from day to day, keeping pace with the intensity of the traffic.[4] The charges on the canals again were nowhere based on cost of service; not only were differences of charge made according to the value of the

[1] Cullom Committee Rep., p. 109.
[2] Eighth Report of Iowa Board of R. R. Commissioners (1885), p. 35.
[3] *Cf.* Aucoc, Les tarif des chemins de fer (1880), p. 43.
[4] De Foville, Transformation des moyens de transport (1880), p. 63.

commodities transported, as on the American and English canals, but in many instances differential rates were charged, although no one thought of opposing them in principle.[1] So the earliest railway acts were based unconsciously on value of service. In the charter of the first English steam railway — the Stockton and Darlington — among other charges which deviate from cost of service we find that rates on coal destined for exportation are fixed at $4d.$ per ton-mile, but on all other coal at $\frac{1}{2}d.$ per ton-mile. Similar distinctions may be found in most of the early charters. In the United States these provisions were not so common, simply because there were very few charter-maxima for freight. But at all events these examples prove that the cost of service principle was by no means avowedly followed. What has been called, even in the official documents the "outrageous principle" or the "audacious plea" of value of service[2] is thus not a new departure. The principle is as old as the improved methods of transportation themselves.

Moreover, the value theory is not so opposed to the cost theory as is frequently imagined. We know that lower rates for cheap (or distant) goods increase the traffic and thus diminish the cost of service. The value of the articles thus affects traffic and cost. And since the reduction of rates for cheap goods leaves only a small surplus above operating expenses for fixed charges, while higher rates affect the dear (or near) goods very little, there is no valid reason why the latter should not be made to bear a proportionately larger share of the fixed charges. From the standpoint of justice no exception can be taken to the principle of value, even regarded as a product of the principle of cost.

But is the doctrine of cost of production itself universally applicable as the foundation of prices? What the railway produces is transportation; its cost of production is cost of service. It is claimed that the utilities produced by the railway, like all

[1] On the Pennsylvania canal there were 12 classes, the rate varying from 0.6 to 4 cents per ton-mile. For Europe, *cf.* Sax, Die Verkehrsmittel (1878), I, 180; Jacqmin, De l'exploitation des chemins de fer (1868), I, 368.

[2] Report of Mass. R. R. Com. (1885), p. 35. *Cf.* the minority view of English Select Com. of 1882, Rep., p. liv.

utilities which are the subject of exchange, should be regulated by cost of production. This, it is asserted, is the only just law. But such a conclusion is of doubtful validity. Even granting that cost of production forms a just basis for prices, no one claims that actual business prices of each particular commodity vary with the cost. The application to railway rates is plain. The cost of service theory might logically demand that the sum total of charges should vary with the cost, but not that the price of each individual transaction should be fixed by its cost of service. Even were this practicable, — which we have seen is not the case, — it would not be theoretically defensible.

The principle of value of service has a firmer foundation. Railway charges cannot, indeed, be fixed like prices in general, simply by demand and supply. This is the mistake of the railway officials who attempt to justify all charges.[1] Railway transportation is more than a simple business; it is a semi-public occupation, a public trust. Hence the necessity of restricting the inequalities of every-day commercial practice. But to oppose the abuses of a principle is quite another thing from demurring to the principle itself. The value-of-service doctrine, correctly understood, simply applies the methods already followed in certain public relations. It fixes charges according to the ability to pay — the same principle that is recognized in taxation. Charging what the traffic will bear is a rough way of stating that the charges are proportioned to the capacity or ability of the articles that compose the traffic. It will not be questioned that the endeavors to develop traffic can be realized only by making lower charges for the cheaper (and distant) goods. But the element of justice is introduced as soon as we show that such a method graduates charges according to ability. Of course it does not follow that all rates actually charged are just rates. The inference simply is that the principle of value, as a principle, is not open to the objections often

---

[1] So de la Gournerie, Études économiques sur l'exploitation des chemins de fer (1880), pp. 118, 119; Grierson, Railway Rates (1886), p. 68; and most of the American writers.

urged. The ability of an article to pay, its capacity to contribute to the payment of the expenses, is an undeniably valid basis for rates. As it is well expressed by the Cullom Committee:

> The capacity of each commodity to contribute to the payment of the fixed charges is measured by the extent to which the cost of its transportation fixes its market value and determines the question of its movement. In the case of commodities like coal, stone, ore, beef, corn, lumber, *etc.*, the freight charge constitutes the principal item of cost to the consumer; however small may be his contribution to the general burden, it is relatively greater than that made by the consumer of high-priced articles, such as clothing or dry goods, *e.g.*, the selling-price of which is not appreciably affected by the freight charges, even though unreasonably high.[1]

And what is true of the cheap goods is true of the distant goods. For the purposes of transportation they stand on precisely the same footing and are subject to the same conditions. The principle again applies equally well to passenger traffic. Even in the United States there are virtually different classes, and the higher fares for the better service may be upheld on the principle that the passengers in the higher class cars possess more ability to pay large fares than those in ordinary or emigrant cars. [The value of service principle is based on supposed ability to pay.]

But now the difficult question arises. We have shown that the low-priced wares possess less ability to pay than the high-priced wares. Does it follow that the more valuable wares, by reason of their greater ability to pay, should be charged higher rates than the average, or than would otherwise be the case, in order to compensate for the lower rates of the cheaper goods? Does the principle of value imply this compensating action, and is this principle of compensation valid and just? This is the puzzling question. To give a precise answer is not so simple as it might appear. We may, indeed, assert with decision that difference in value implies a difference in ability to pay, but it is rather arbitrary and hazardous to assert exactly what relation

[1] Report, p. 185.

there is between value and ability. Shall an article of double the value pay twice the rate; and if not, why not? The difficulty, in fact, is exactly the same that is met with in the problems of taxation. One of the fundamental principles of equity in taxation is that contributors should pay taxes in proportion to their ability. A rich man ought to pay more than a poor man; the difficulty arises when we must determine exactly how much more he ought to pay. Is the difference of ability proportional to their property, or to their income, or to their expenses? Or, again, should the difference of ability be measured not by a proportional, but by a progressive, scale of taxation, — should there be a progressive property, or a progressive income, or a progressive expense tax, rather than a proportional tax? None of these questions can be declared definitely settled by the science of finance. The answers are necessarily vague because of the relativity in the test of ability.

Exactly the same considerations are applicable to railway tariffs. Difference in value implies difference in ability. The cheap articles possess less ability than the dear goods, and should thus pay lower rates. But to determine how much higher rates the others should pay is not a self-evident proposition. The question is a relative one, and the rates may vary within wide limits. It is precisely because the question is a relative one that the many abuses of railway management have arisen. This relativity, the possibility of making undue differences within the limits of the just principle, becomes therefore a strong argument in favor of some form of public regulation.[1] The unhampered railway management may pursue the correct policy of charging what they think the service is worth, but their opinions may vary within wide limits. There is, in other words, such a possible elasticity or flexibility in the methods of fixing the details that the actual charges may be far from adequately satisfying all demands. This fact above all others has earned for the doctrine of charging what the traffic will bear the deserved

---

[1] Cohn, Untersuchungen über die englische Eisenbahnpolitik, Bd. iii (1883), S. 84, concludes that the railways must therefore be owned and managed by the state. But such a conclusion is not at all necessary.

epithet of "hap-hazard" estimate.[1] The doctrine of free competition and uncontrolled liberty does not follow from the principle of value of service as the foundation of railway tariffs.

But at all events one point has been gained. The principle of value, within these wide limits, is a principle which not only does determine railway tariffs, but which, although liable to abuse, is a correct principle. It is just because it is founded on the principle of ability. It is neither new nor "outrageous." It is not only a just principle, but, as we have seen, the only practicable principle. The cost of service doctrine can no longer put forth the exclusive claim of justice as the basis of railway tariffs.

One exaggeration, however, must be avoided. The principle of value, we said, implies the doctrine of compensation. But this does not imply that the higher charges on the dear goods or local traffic are higher than they would be if there were no lower charges on the cheap goods or through traffic. Were the rates on the cheap or long-distance traffic to be raised, it would not be transported at all; and since its contribution to the fixed expenses would fall away, the whole expense would necessarily be borne by the dear and short-distance traffic. The rates on the latter would have to be increased to make good for the loss of the former; the dear and local freight would pay even more than it pays now. Those who object to the principle of value because it unduly raises the charges on high-class and local business thus utterly fail to perceive that in many cases it produces just the contrary effect. The principle of value often lowers the rates on the dear goods, and renders possible the transportation of the cheap goods. It is the long-distance traffic which has enabled the American railways to reduce their charges, through as well as local, far below the level of European tariffs. *Pro rata* charges, or even rates based solely on cost of service, would give us tariffs much higher than those in actual use; they would level up, not level down.

Classification and differential rates are thus legitimate and necessary expedients: legitimate, because based on value; neces-

[1] Sir B. Samuelson, Report on Railway Goods Tariffs, *etc.* (1886), p. 20.

sary, because without them railway transportation would become vastly less efficient. The same analysis would show the illegitimacy of personal discriminations, even in wholesale transactions. [Classification and local discrimination reduce rates for the traffic which is less able to pay; personal discrimination reduces rates for the traffic which is better able to pay. Reduced rates to large shippers increase the advantages of the strong; rates fixed according to value tend to diminish the disadvantages of the weak.] Preferential rates are wrong because not based on the principle of value; differential rates are right because following the doctrine of value. Preferential rates invert the considerations of ability; differential rates maintain the principle of ability.

But we must not be misunderstood. While the principle of charging what the traffic will bear is essentially just and legitimate from the railway standpoint, from the public standpoint it must be regarded as a subordinate principle. Value of service puts into the hands of the railways practically a power of taxation. It is indeed not entirely an arbitrary power, since the charges are partially regulated by water competition. But in its essence it is a power of taxation — a taxation often cunningly masked in the methods of classification and discrimination. From the public standpoint we maintain the great principle of equal treatment for all persons and all business. This is the general rule; the principle of value must be viewed as a legitimate qualification of the rule of equal treatment. But it must be shown in every particular case that the service *is* of varying value. From the public standpoint in other words the burden of proof must rest on the railways. (Charging what the traffic will bear is just, but its application is so elastic that the justice must be demonstrated in each instance.) To leave the application of the principle to the discretion of the railway results in the chaotic, almost barbaric, condition of actual charges during railway wars. The only rational method to reconcile public and private interests is to lay down the rule of equal treatment for all persons and places, and to admit the principle of value as a necessary infraction of the rule. But the necessity of the infraction must be shown before its legitimacy is accepted. The principle of differential rates is just; all differential rates are not just.

The question hence arises: How far are these differential rates allowable; to what extent should local discrimination be practised? We are confronted, in other words, by the problem of the long haul versus the short haul, the through traffic versus the local traffic. If we take a line with its two termini as competitive centres, and a third point intermediate between the two, and not subject to the same competition, we may have three principal forms of differential rates:

1. The rate per ton-mile from New York to Buffalo may be less than the rate per ton-mile from New York to Rochester, and yet the aggregate charge to Buffalo may be greater than the aggregate charge to Rochester.

2. The rate per ton-mile from New York to Buffalo may more than cover mere movement expenses, and yet be so much less than the rate per ton-mile from New York to Rochester that the aggregate charge to Buffalo may be slightly less than the aggregate charge to Rochester.

3. The rate per ton-mile from New York to Buffalo may be so low that it will not even cover actual movement expenses, and the aggregate charge to Buffalo will be considerably less than the aggregate charge to Rochester.

The third case occasions but little embarrassment. Such a practice manifestly cannot be defended even from the standpoint of sound railway practice. For new or through business, as we saw, any rate above the additional cost of the new business is a paying rate. It is defensible on the theory of value, because it contributes to the fixed expenses and thus diminishes the burden or rate on the old business. But if the rate falls below the expense of the additional business, it undoubtedly becomes a losing rate. It contributes nothing to fixed expenses, but actually requires an additional charge on the old business to make good the fixed expenses. The justification of differential rates thus entirely falls away. No theory of value can require one shipment to be charged unduly high rates in order to transport another shipment at less than actual cost. This would carry the principle of compensation beyond all reasonable bounds. The only possible exception from the railway standpoint would be to reduce rates temporarily below cost of service in order to build up a certain locality, and thus ultimately develop paying traffic. The present loss may create a future gain. But from the public standpoint this would be inadmissible. To raise local rates in order to decrease rates to competitive points below additional cost of the new business is theoretically indefensible. The minimum rate should never fall below the movement expenses. Any differential rate below this point is illegitimate, and, we may add, comparatively rare, because disastrous to the railway.

We come to the second case, where a higher aggregate charge is made for the short haul than for the long haul. At first blush such a practice seems a flagrant offence. We are tempted to exclaim: This inverts the natural order of things; it must be stopped at all hazards. But the matter is not quite so simple.

It is maintained that lower charges on short hauls remove the geographical advantages of localities, and since the termini of a road are generally larger cities, tend to unduly increase the advantages of the large as against the small places. The same argument, however, is applicable, although in a slighter degree, to any differential rates. They all discriminate against some localities in favor of others. For the purposes of the argument we may treat all differential rates together.

It may indeed be confessed that differential rates do sometimes remove geographical advantages. But it does not follow that such a practice is always reprehensible. There is no such thing as a natural, inviolable geographical advantage. There are no vested rights in situation. One town may be connected with the coast only by a turnpike; another town further distant may have the good fortune to see a railway built through its limits. Has the former any cause to complain because it is robbed of the benefits of its hitherto advantageous situation? A village ten miles distant from a metropolis has been supplying it with garden-produce. Is there any essential injustice in allowing villages forty or fifty miles distant to compete for the same market — a competition possible only through differential rates? In fact, the object of all improved means of transportation is to annihilate distance, to minimize the differences of situation. Maintenance of original differences of situation implies equal mileage rates. It would render impossible all but local business in the vast mass of commodities; it would again turn our western fields into barren wastes. Differential rates widen the field of supply; they increase the specialization of wants, and create the possibility of satisfying these wants, so characteristic of modern industrial society. Opposition to local discrimination arises from viewing solely the interests of the producer; rational economics lead us to consider also the consumer. Opposition to differential rates is based on the supposed welfare of a particular class or section of producers; a wise national economy will ponder over the interests of the whole community, over the prosperity of the entire country, irrespective of sectional jealousies. If differential rates are so arranged that distant producers are enabled to compete with local producers, the latter indeed may see their profits curtailed, but the former will see their profits increased, and the consuming public as a whole will evidently gain.[1] There is no absolute proprietary right in situation.

The charge, again, that differential rates increase the advantages of large cities may be admitted, but without any necessary imputation of injustice. It may be urged that differential rates do not at all differ from preferential rates; that all personal discriminations are wrong because they increase the advantages of the large shipper, and that all local discriminations are wrong because they increase the advantages of the large city. But such an analogy is essentially defective. Two or more shippers have a positive right to equal treatment. A common carrier must not assume the privilege of deciding between them. The common law and common justice demand

---

[1] *Cf.* the recent complaints of California producers and manufacturers at being shut out of Eastern markets by the operation of the Interstate Commerce act.

equality of treatment for similar services. But in the case of localities there is no such indefeasible right. Differential rates which increase the advantages of large cities are due simply to the fact that these cities are competitive centres. The discrimination is the result of the competition. To avoid the discrimination, you must avert the competition, whether by rail or water. The building of an additional line temporarily increases the advantages of the terminus,[1] for every new railway alters in some degree the relative advantages of situation. The local points simply pay the penalty of not being competitive points, and to accord all local points the same benefits as competitive points would be to invert the normal development. Differential rates in such cases maintain the natural advantages of situation, while *pro rata* charges would here invert the geographical advantages. Equality between persons is rightfully demanded because the services are similar; equality between places is not always necessary, because the services are sometimes dissimilar. The ability of long-distance freight to bear the charges diminishes faster than the distance increases.[2]

But of course this view does not justify all differential rates. The abuses have often been outrageous, the methods undeserving of palliation. Local interests have been disregarded, and the discriminations so conducted as to ruin whole businesses or towns in order to build up others. It is not necessary to ascribe illicit motives to the railway managers, although even such examples have not been wanting in our history. They

---

[1] Temporarily, *i.e.*, until some combination is effected between the rival lines; and such a combination is sure to ensue in the shape of a pool, an arrangement, or a consolidation. If there is water or foreign competition, the effect may be permanent instead of temporary.

[2] The English courts at first interpreted Cardwell's Traffic act of 1854 in the above sense. The clause reads: "No company shall make or give any undue or unreasonable preference or advantage to, or in favor of, any particular person or company, or any particular description of traffic in any respect whatsoever." The courts held that this demand for equality of treatment applies only to persons; but that nothing prevents the railways from favoring one class of traders, or one town, or one portion of their traffic, provided the conditions are the same for all persons, and for the benefit of the railway. See the decisions in Shelford, Law of Railways (4th ed.), I, 166–174. *Cf.* also the English Parliamentary Report for 1872 (Joint Select Committee on Railway Companies Amalgamation), p. xiii.

have often been forced into unjust discrimination by the stress of competition and the instinct of self-preservation. But railway officials commit a great mistake in calling all local discriminations just because they are the effect of competition, precisely as the demagogues err in opposing undeniably valid discriminations and at the same time upholding competition. Competition is made to cover a multitude of sins. From the standpoint of railway profits, all actual differential rates, unless where railways carry at less than hauling expenses, may indeed be defensible; but from the public standpoint of national prosperity and the equable development of all sections, many of them may easily be convicted of injustice.[1] Railway profits and public interests do not always go hand in hand. The possible diversity of interest renders some form of governmental supervision absolutely imperative. Untrammelled liberty has been tried in the balance and found wanting. Private actions which so materially affect public interests must be subject to review and correction at the hands of some public authority.

The main limitation on the practice of differential rates hitherto has been the enactment of short-haul laws.

The short-haul system admits differential rates, but prescribes that the aggregate charge to any intermediate point shall not exceed the aggregate charge to the final point; the entire distance must never be charged less than any part of it. As a principle, it is in itself legitimate. It tends to check the undue extension of the practice of differential rates. For although, as we have seen, there is no vested interest in geographical advantages, it becomes an anomaly to charge to a way-station the rate

---

[1] Thus Alexander, Railway Practice (1887), p. 14, says: "The competition which gives birth to such discriminations determines also their sizes, or the extent to which they must go. What are the rates to intermediate points has nothing to do with the case." Expressed in this general way, the principle is manifestly indefensible, for it would justify transportation to competitive centres at less than actual hauling expenses. It must be remembered that railway profits are no excuse for injustice to the public. So Fink, Argument before Senate Committee on the Reagan Bill (1879), p. 20, claims that competition would justify a charge of $1.50 a ton from A to B, and of $3.00 from A to an intermediate point, C. It is these exaggerated claims that arouse the ire of the public. For the claims of the railway antagonists in England, see Pope, Railway Rates and Radical Rule (1884).

to a competing point further on, plus the additional rate from the competing point back to the way-station. This amounts, in fact, to making an extra charge for *not* transporting the goods to a more distant place.[1] Put in this way, the hardship is apparent. As a general rule, the short-haul principle should be followed.

But a categorical and absolute prohibition of charging more for the short-haul would be of dubious value. If the law could be applied to all media of transportation, waterways as well as railways, foreign as well as home railways, then the matter would be simplified. But as long as such competition exists, the anomalies cannot be entirely removed. The attempt to do so by law would simply decrease the profits of the railway without improving the condition of the public. New York and New Orleans are connected by water as well as by rail. The railway charges cannot exceed the water rates by more than a definite amount, even though such charges only give a slight profit above movement expenses, and by no means cover the total cost of service. The charges to New Orleans are less than to an intermediate point, X. What would be the effect of a short-haul law? Rates to X would be lowered, or New Orleans rates would be increased. If rates to X are lowered, the profits of the railway will be seriously curtailed, and it is questionable whether it could defray its expenses at all. The railway will hence far prefer to raise the New Orleans rates, as on the whole less injurious. If New Orleans rates are raised, the water lines will take all the traffic, and the rates to X will have to be increased still more. For the railway will now have no New Orleans business to contribute to its fixed expenses, and will have to meet these by the proceeds of the local business alone. The local discrimination would hence be increased, for actual rates to New Orleans by water remain as before. No one will gain except the steamship company.

What is true of New Orleans is true of all points subject to water competition, or influenced through their connection by water competition. The same considerations apply to the com-

[1] *Cf.* Adams, Railroads, their Origin and Problems (1879), p. 124.

petition of foreign railways. A short-haul law applicable to the United States but not to Canada would simply transfer the profits of the American railways to the Canadian, without decreasing the local discriminations.

Here again the principle is correct, but the exact application a matter of difficulty. It is a conflict between railway profits and impartial justice. If the short-haul principle in any given case decreases profits, but not to such an extent as to virtually ruin or handicap the railway, then it may safely be applied. In many cases the lowering of local rates would not have this baneful result, for the reason that the main traffic of the railway is the through traffic. This explains why many railways are now reducing their local charges. The short-haul principle will not materially affect their earnings. But in many other cases the above examples will hold good. The through rates will have to be advanced, and the railways will suffer without any benefits to the public, or, in fact, to any one but the rival transportation agencies. Both railway officials and railway antagonists are hence wrong. The demagogues are wrong because they fail to see the limitations of the short-haul principle; the railway officials are wrong because they set forth competition as a reason for all existing infractions of the principle. Competition becomes a valid reason only where the short-haul system implies a necessary choice between ruinous curtailment of profits and complete loss of the business. The limit is an elastic one, and precisely on this account do we need some public authority to define the justice of the limit in each particular case. But an inflexible law, enforcing the short-haul principle in all cases, would be neither wise nor successful.

Prior to the enactment of the Interstate Commerce act, several states already had short-haul laws on the statute books. According to the Commutation of Tonnage act of 1861, a contract between the state of Pennsylvania and the Pennsylvania Railroad Company, the short-haul provision was agreed to. But neither this agreement nor the law of 1883, which incorporated the same principle, was ever thoroughly carried out.[1] The

[1] *Cf.* the testimony of Pennsylvania shippers in Cullom Rep., Test. (Norris), pp. 530–535, (Welsh) p. 460, (Wood) pp. 478–480, *etc.*

Granger movement of 1870–1875 resulted in the passage of very stringent laws in the Western States, some of them being virtually *pro rata* laws. Many of the specifically short-haul laws, as that of 1873 in Ohio, remained dead letters, while the more stringent laws, which absolutely fixed rates or empowered the commissioners to fix rates, were enforced so literally as to produce a revulsion in public feeling and a speedy repeal of the laws.[1] The same is true of the more recent short-haul laws in the North-west, as, *e.g.*, the Doane law of 1881 in Nebraska. The railways enforced it so strictly by raising local rates that the public began to regard it as a burden, not a relief. As a result, the law is now practically a dead letter.[2] Several of these laws were, however, something more than mere short-haul laws. They provided, in general, that a shorter distance should not be charged more than a longer distance on the same line, while according to a true short-haul law the shorter distance must be included within the longer distance. This distinction was well expressed in the Massachusetts law of 1874, which reads as follows:

No railroad corporation shall charge or receive for the transportation of freight to any station on its road a greater sum than is at the time charged or received for the transportation of the like class and quantity of freight *from the same original point of departure* to a station at a greater distance on its road *in the same direction*.[3]

But this law, as the phraseology denotes, applies only to hauls from a terminus to the way-stations. It does not apply in the other direction, *i.e.*, from the way-stations to the terminus. Possibly on this account, but probably because of the smaller degree of competitive traffic in the state, it has been found possible to enforce the law strictly.[4]

The New York commission made a careful study of the principle in 1884. Their conclusion is expressed in these words:[5]

---

[1] So in Wisconsin, Iowa, Michigan, Minnesota.
[2] Cullom Committee Report, Test. (Rosewater), pp. 1133–34.
[3] Public Statutes, chap. 112, § 190.
[4] Railroad Commissioners' Report, 1885, and 1886, p. 35, *in re* Housatonic Railroad Co. See also Cullom Rep., Test. (Russell), p. 305.
[5] Report on the *pro rata* bill (1884), p. 120.

Railroads should not as a general rule charge more between a terminal and an intermediate point, for a like class and quantity of freight, than is charged between such terminal and a more distant point, even though at such more distant point there may be railroad or water competition, unless railroads can affirmatively establish such circumstances governing such competition as justify the higher charge for the shorter distance.

This is a conservative and judicious conclusion, which shuts out on the one hand the extravagant claims of the railway officials, and on the other the short-sighted demands of the professional reformers. Each case must be judged on its own merits. Thus in Moon *vs.* The New York, Ontario and Western,[1] competition with a rival railway was held not sufficient to justify the infraction of the principle. In Foot *et al. vs.* The Utica and Black River,[2] it was held that higher charges might sometimes be made to intermediate points, but that the peculiar circumstances were not sufficient in this case. In Harding and Hollis *vs.* Rome, Watertown, and Oswego,[3] water competition, which would have given the business to foreign companies, was held to be a valid reason for the infraction of the rule. The short-haul principle as administered in New York is thus no hard and fast rule.

European experience all tends to the same result. In France the short-haul principle is known as the *clause des stations non dénommées*, and has been in force since 1864. The railway tariffs must be submitted to the administration, and in virtue of this power of approval or *homologation*, the government has procured the insertion and maintenance of the short-haul principle.[4] But this is applicable only to the general tariffs, and is perfectly enforceable there because of the almost utter absence of interior competition — a fact due to the existence of territorialization or division of the field among the separate companies. The principle is not applicable to any case where

---

[1] N. Y. Railroad Commissioners' Report (1885), pp. 73-76.
[2] Report (1884), pp. 94-131, especially pp. 106 and 119.
[3] Report (1884), p. 160.
[4] Aucoc, Conférences sur le droit administratif (2ᵐᵉ éd., 1882), III, 748. *Cf.* Picard, Chemins de fer français (1885), II, 444; III, 587.

there is any danger of foreign competition. The *tarifs de transit*, or through tariffs for goods passing through France on the way to another state, and the *tarifs d'exportation*, or through rates for goods destined for exportation, are exempted from the application of the principle, so that greater charges are permitted to intermediate points. This, it must be remembered, is allowed by public authority and in the public interest.[1]

In Germany, where the railways are almost exclusively owned by the state governments, and interior competition thus minimized, there is likewise no hard and fast rule. The short-haul principle, or *Princip der hintergelegenen Stationen*, is accepted as a general rule in Prussia, but exceptions may be admitted by the minister of public works.[2] The Bundesrath of the empire also enunciated the same principle, but expressly inserted the proviso that particular circumstances might justify an infraction of the rule.[3] These exceptions are of frequent occurrence.[4] The short-haul principle does not apply to through-transit rates, to import or export tariffs, or to any competitive centres where the competition is caused by waterways or foreign railways. After the purchase of the Prussian railways by the state a few years ago, the attempt was made to enforce the short-haul rule strictly, but it ignominiously failed.[5] The *Seehafen-Ausnahme-Tarif*, and a large number of other special rates permit charges in derogation of the short-haul principle. Even the earnest defenders of state railways confess that numerous exceptions are indispensable.[6]

In Switzerland the short-haul principle is maintained in a recent report of the Diet, but exceptions are permitted in the

---

[1] The accounts of European practice in the New York Commission Report on the *pro rata* bill are inexact and untrustworthy.
[2] *Cf.* the ministerial rescripts in Krönig, Die Differentialtarife der Eisenbahnen.
[3] Bundesrath, Sitzung vom 6. April, 1877.
[4] "Ziemlich häufig" is the phrase used by a prominent German official in a letter to me. The matter is decided in every case " auf Grund der jedesmal vorliegenden thatsächlichen Verhältnisse."
[5] *Cf.* especially the test. of Forbes in English Select Committee Rep. (1882). Evid. 169 *et seq.*
[6] Ulrich, Eisenbahn-Tarifwesen (1886), pp. 150–152.

case of foreign competition.[1] In Austria the short-haul clause is inserted in many of the railway charters, but both in the state and in the private lines the exceptions are exceedingly numerous.[2] In Belgium and Holland, where the laws literally interpreted enjoin mileage rates, the vast majority of actual charges are arranged according to special rates, many of which permit greater charges for the shorter distances.[3] In Italy similar special rates may be approved by the government.[4] Thus in no country where the tariffs are fixed by the state or subject to public control is the short-haul principle an absolute rule.

In England, indeed, the short-haul principle has been affirmed by the courts,[5] and the railway commission has of late gone even further in its opposition to differential rates. In the celebrated Broughton and Plas Power Coal Company case it was held that the charge for the longer distance must not only be greater than for the shorter distance, but must actually more than suffice to cover the total cost of the extra service.[6] But these decisions have had very little influence on the actual arrangements of tariffs in Great Britain, and have been severely criticised in the parliamentary commissions.[7] The decisions, moreover, are by no means uniform, and in a very recent case it was held by the court that differential rates are perfectly legitimate if in the one case the rate is a local rate, and in the other simply a portion of a through rate.[8] It is not "under sub-

[1] Bericht des Bundesrathes an die Bundesversammlung, Nov. 23, 1883; in Hürlimann, Die eidgenössische Eisenbahngesetzgebung (1887).

[2] Schreiber, Das Tarifwesen der Eisenbahnen (1884), S. 181, 191, 199. *Cf.* Nördling, Die Selbstkosten des Eisenbahntransports (1885), S. 219.

[3] Jacqmin, Étude sur les chemins de fer des Pays-bas (1882), p. 87; Nicolai, Les chemins de fer de l'État en Belgique (1885), p. 29.

[4] Agreements of 1885 with the Mediterranean lines, cap. 4, § 39, 44.

[5] *Cf.* Budd *vs.* London and Northwestern Railway Co., 36 L. T. N. S. 802. This was a case of sea competition. The decision was opposed to the principle of the older decisions under Cardwell's act.

[6] Railway Commission, Tenth Report (1883).

[7] Select Com. (1882), Evidence, pp. 71, 89; especially the celebrated cases of Evershed and the Denaby main.

[8] Hull, Barnaby and West Riding Junction Railway *vs.* Yorkshire and Derbyshire Coal Co.

stantially similar circumstances." Lord Stanley's bill of 1887 in fact expressly provides that the justice of differential rates should be measured by the necessity of securing the traffic.[1]

We are thus prepared to pass an opinion on the Interstate Commerce law. The short-haul clause reads as follows:

> That it shall be unlawful for any common carrier subject to the provisions of this act to charge or receive any greater compensation in the aggregate for the transportation of passengers or of like kind of property, under substantially similar circumstances and conditions, for a shorter than for a longer distance over the same line, in the same direction, the shorter being included within the longer distance. . . . Provided, however, that upon application to the commission appointed under the provisions of this act, such common carrier may in special cases, after investigation by the commission, be authorized to charge less for longer than for shorter distances for the transportation of passengers or property; and the commission may, from time to time, prescribe the extent to which such designated common carrier may be relieved from the operation of this section of this act.

It is improbable that the commission will interpret the act in the sense that the words "under substantially similar circumstances and conditions" justify all existing differential rates due to competition. This would practically emasculate the law. But on the other hand an analysis of the principles of rates and the results of European experience have shown us that any attempt to apply the law in all cases would be ruinous. A strict enforcement of the short-haul clause would most certainly result in general discontent and a speedy repeal. The safety-valve consists in the discretion afforded to the commissioners, and upon them the success or failure of the law depends. The act is an expression of a correct principle, but the limitations of the principle are no less obvious. The country is to be congratulated on the legislative recognition of the rule; let us trust that there may be equal cause for congratulation on the official recognition of its limitations.

Our preliminary conclusion may now be formulated. Under a system of free competition among private railways the

[1] Railway and Canal Traffic bill, § 25, sec. 2.

principle of value of service or charging what the traffic will bear is the only rational method, calculated to give the most efficient service and the greatest profits. But the existence or possibility of the abuse of power requires the restriction of this unlimited liberty in the public interest. The reconciliation of the railways and the public can take place only through the interposition of public authority. The public authority must lay down the rule of equal treatment as the fundamental doctrine, but must recognize the principle of value as a reason for departing from the doctrine in any individual case. Omission of either duty necessarily entails injustice or inefficiency. The short-haul clause is a partial recognition of the demand for equal treatment; the discretion given the commission is implicitly a partial recognition of the theory of value. The Interstate Commerce act thus accepts the principle and concedes its limitations; in this respect at least it is a wise and judicious measure. For the commission to ignore the limitations in the attempt to realize the principle would be an act of consummate folly.

EDWIN R. A. SELIGMAN.

RAILWAY TARIFFS AND THE INTERSTATE COMMERCE LAW.

II.

SCARCELY second in importance to the short-haul clause of the national law, which has been discussed in the preceding essay,[1] is the section which prohibits pooling. What is the true significance of pooling? What will be the effect of the law? To give a correct answer we must enter upon a consideration of competition in general.

And here we are immediately confronted by the two fundamental questions: Is free competition universally beneficent? Is free competition universally existent?

The doctrine of free competition is essentially a modern idea.

---

[1] POLITICAL SCIENCE QUARTERLY, June, 1887, p. 223. It has been a source of great satisfaction to me that the Interstate Commerce commission in its recent weighty decision has taken substantially the same ground as that occupied in my first article. The chief points are as follows:

"*First.* That the prohibition in the fourth section against a greater charge for a shorter than for a longer distance . . . is limited to cases in which the circumstances and conditions are substantially similar.

"*Third.* That . . . in case of complaint for violating the fourth section the burden of proof is on the carrier.

"*Fifth.* That the existence of actual competition . . . may make out the dissimilar circumstances and conditions . . . in the following cases:

1. When the competition is with carriers by water which are not subject to the provisions of the statute.

2. When the competition is with foreign or other railroads which are not subject to the provisions of the statute.

3. In rare and peculiar cases of competition between railroads which are subject to the statute, where a strict application of the general rule of the statute would be destructive of legitimate competition.

"*Sixth.* . . . The fact that long-haul traffic will only bear certain rates is no reason for carrying it for less than cost at the expense of other traffic." — *In re* The Louisville & Nashville R.R. Co. *et al.*, pp. 27–29.

As the basis of nineteenth century economics it was first formulated by the Physiocrats and Adam Smith. It is entirely foreign to ancient and mediæval conceptions. The economy of the middle ages was founded on the idea of reasonable, customary price — the *justum pretium* of the legists, theologians, and statesmen. The institutions were based on restrictions, privileges, and enforced monopolies, while the legislative prohibitions were not entirely the product of class selfishness but in part the recognized expression of an attempt to secure distributive justice. That the legislators finally overreached themselves and stifled all liberty by their multifarious restrictions is a well-known fact. The necessary and salutary reaction found its theoretic justification in the "natural law" tenets of the eighteenth century, and a partial realization of those tenets followed in the first half of the nineteenth century. The idea now became current that a reign of free competition and its logical correlative, absolute *laissez faire*, would bring about a harmony of interests, a state of universal bliss. The enthusiasm of Bastiat and McCulloch was natural in seeing the world break away from the shackles of mediæval restraint. But recent experience has demonstrated the falsity of their anticipations and has disclosed serious defects in the *régime* of free competition. It does not always work evenly; it often secures undue advantages to the unscrupulous; it has given birth to great abuses in the factory system and the fraudulent speculation of modern society. The law of competition is not always beneficent.

Furthermore, it does not exist universally. The doctrine depends on the postulates of absolute transferability of labor and capital. But this assumption is approximately true in only a few instances, absolutely untrue in many instances. In the industrial undertakings of the present day the capital invested is often fixed, not circulating, capital, and cannot easily be transferred to a more lucrative business. It is difficult to gauge even approximately the superior profitableness of some competitive enterprise; and even when it has been gauged, it is still more difficult at once to transfer the capital. In fact, in only one department of business life does the doctrine of the absolute play of free competition hold good — in the stock exchange of modern times.¹

John Stuart Mill long ago called attention to what we may term economic or industrial monopolies, where competition is neither illegal nor absolutely shut out by nature, but where it is shown to be practically undesirable and utterly inefficient, thus of itself giving place to some form of monopoly.² Other writers, and especially Farrer,³ have attempted to analyze these phenomena and show why the law of competition is not applicable. Certain characteristics are common to them all. The industry demands a large amount of capital; it supplies a necessary of life; the article furnished is local; the industry occupies a peculiarly favored situation; the method of operation requires unity and harmony of management; the production can be largely increased without a proportionate increase of capital. This is true not only of docks, waterworks, and gasworks, but of all media of transportation — turnpikes, canals, telegraph, post, and railways. In some of these competition has never been attempted; in most cases it has been tried, but has miserably failed. The disappearance of competition has benefited the companies and in many instances also the public. But at all events, whether beneficial or not, competition has disappeared, and combination and monopoly have resulted.

The chief consideration is the possibility of increased production without proportionate increase of plant or capital. To use a happy phrase, the business is subject to the law of increasing returns.⁴ The traffic on a railroad may be doubled without the necessity of duplicating roadbed, track, terminals, and general expenses. Ten lines between New York and Albany would not benefit the public, and would certainly ruin

---

[1] This explains, as Cohn pointed out, why Ricardo, who was a stock-exchange broker, first successfully elaborated the theory of free competition. Untersuchungen über die englische Eisenbahnpolitik, Bd. II (1875), S. 384.

[2] Book v, ch. xi, § 11; Appleton's ed. 1880, vol. ii, p. 584.

[3] *Cf.* Industrial Monopolies, *Quarterly Review*, October, 1870. Also Sax, Die Verkehrsmittel, Bd. I, S. 66 *et seq.*, and Simon Sterne, Monopolies, Lalor's Cyclopædia of Political Science, vol. ii.

[4] H. C. Adams, Relation of the State to Industrial Action, Publications of the American Economic Association, vol. 1 (1887), p. 523.

each other. One line judiciously managed can perform all the work at far less cost. The railway is an economic monopoly; the inevitable tendency is toward fusion and single-headed management.

In addition to these economic monopolies proper, we find almost every department of wholesale trade at present taking the form of industrial combination. To maintain that prices are everywhere regulated by the free play of competition is no longer permissible. We cannot ignore the fact that producers find it to their interest to combine and agree on certain prices less than which it shall be unlawful to ask or take. Adam Smith already said: "People of the same trade hardly meet together even for merriment and diversion, but the conversation ends in a conspiracy against the public, or in some contrivance to raise prices." Even then the movement had begun; to-day it has become well-nigh universal. There is scarcely a trade throughout the land without its combinations,— many of which in the last few months have taken the impalpable form of trusts, in the endeavor to attain corporate advantages without assuming corporate responsibilities. There are really four classes: combinations to limit production, to regulate prices, to regulate distribution, to divide the field. Some comprise all four characteristics. To describe or enumerate them is needless in view of the recent discussions to which they have been subjected.[1] But the facts exist. Prices are no longer determined by the action of free competition, but by the artificial manipulation of these industrial combinations or partial monopolies.

Are these combinations now a necessary evil? Are they an evil at all? Here it will be necessary to revise our natural opinion that monopoly is always injurious. This is as great a mistake as to affirm that competition is always beneficent. The characteristic feature of modern economy is that articles are produced not to satisfy any particular demand, but for the world

[1] *Cf.* J. B. Clark, Limits of Competition, and F. H. Giddings, Persistence of Competition, POLITICAL SCIENCE QUARTERLY, March, 1887, pp. 45, 62. Also the articles of H. D. Lloyd, *North American Review*, 1884 and 1885. For Europe, see Kleinwächter, Die Kartelle (1883). For England, Select Committee on Railways (1882), Evid. qu. 3893; (1881), Evid. qu. 16,376.

market. Unregulated production, production uncontrolled by the state of the market, overproduction or mistaken production have brought about the modern commercial crises. A period of large profits alternating with a period of large losses, extremely low prices alternating with extremely high prices, — this has been the history of modern industry. It is a period of industrial anarchy.

Combinations are designed to put an end to this anarchy. They do away with the excessive fluctuations of prices, performing much the same function as legitimate speculation. Of course, in most cases, they have only their own profits in view; but is it true, as Adam Smith thought, that they are always a conspiracy against the public? A careful analysis must lead us to answer no. They better their own condition, but in so doing they often better the public condition. Steadiness of price is better than fitful fluctuations in price; regulation of production is better than the underproduction or overproduction which results in crises; combination is preferable to "cut-throat" competition which ruins the producer without benefiting the public.

It is of course undeniable that there are possible or actual abuses connected with these combinations. But from this simply results the necessity of public control. We have the alternative: Leave the combinations alone or regulate them. There is no third method. We may prohibit them, but we cannot prevent them. If we make them illegal, we shall simply make them secret. We cannot prevent two men from agreeing not to compete with each other. Robert Stephenson truly said, in 1853: "Where combination is possible, competition is impossible."[1] The whole trend of modern development is to substitute the large for the small, to put combination in the place of competition. We cannot stop the progress; we must recognize it.

The question thus arises: Shall we allow these associations

---

[1] This phrase was not coined by George Stephenson, as Hadley, Railroad Transportation, p. 66, erroneously asserts, but by his son Robert. *Cf.* Report Select Committee on Railway and Canal Bills (1853), Evid. qu. 885, 886, p. 92. This is a mistake almost universally made.

to develop as they will, or is it the duty of the public to interpose its authority and to regulate what it cannot prevent? Put in these words, the answer seems plain. We must recognize the monopolies as existing facts but hold them under control. We have in general gone on the opposite theory. We have believed in the universal existence and beneficence of free competion; we have wilfully blinded our eyes to what was taking place about us; and to-day we wake up only to recognize the existence of these gigantic combinations. To legislate against them and fall back again on the specific of free competition would be absolutely futile. Competition has had its day and has proved ineffective. Let us be bold enough to look the facts straight in the face and not shrink from the logical conclusions of our premises. Recognize the combinations but regulate them.

The application of all this to railways is plain. As a regulator of charges, competition between railways is even less effective than in other large occupations. The doctrine of transferability of capital, partially true elsewhere, is absolutely false here. The railway possesses all the elements of a practical monopoly. So obvious are the advantages of agreement and fusion, that whenever a railway system has started out with competition of independent lines it has inevitably resulted in some form of combination. The public has profited no less than the companies. The curse of free trade in railways has been the system of parallel and often needless lines. An additional road between two terminal points frequently represents so much wasted capital, and the necessity of earning profits on this swollen capital simply aggravates the burden on the public. No more serious blunder has been made than to suppose that increased competition means increased facilities and lower charges. The competition, while it lasts, is of a desperate character, and each line strains itself to the utmost to obtain the business which is only sufficient for one. Charges indeed may be lowered temporarily, but the strenuous attempt to procure the traffic gives birth to the very worst abuses of railway management — secret personal discriminations and immoderate local discriminations. The changes are violent, the conditions unstable. Reduction of rates is sometimes carried to such a point that not even operating expenses are met, for the reckless and bankrupt roads feel no need of earning any fixed charges. The railway wars, which are the logical and extreme manifestations of railway competition, thus exhaust the companies and afford but a dubious relief to the public. Lowness of charges is outweighed by the instability of charges. And the reduction itself is necessarily of an ephemeral character. Continuance of the rates means universal bankruptcy; escape from ruin is possible only through combination. The combination which results again raises rates, and the charges must now be sufficient to earn profits on the often increased capital of the two lines. If competition be beneficial to the public, it is a very temporary benefit; if railway wars, on the other hand, throw all trade into confusion and engender the most aggravated abuses, then the cessation of the competition is a boon to the public, even though the combination results in a relative increase of charges. And if this be true, then a railway policy which obviates the danger of railway wars and "cut-throat" competition can give the public not only stability of rates but also the additional advantage of relatively lower charges.

However the railways start out, they are sure to end in combination. It is the same development as in all other economic monopolies, with the sole difference that the railway monopoly is more pronounced and the railway combinations more widespread. In no business are the effects of spasmodic competition more pernicious. It needs but slight acquaintance with the practical construction of railway rates to perceive the absolute interdependence of tariffs. A war between two important lines necessarily involves the interests of distant roads throughout the country. The only escape from ruin is the replacement of competition by some form of combination. No less than seven possible forms of arrangement have been successively tried: 1. Agreement to make equal rates or give equal facilities as to speed, accommodation, *etc*. 2. Agreement to forward traffic over each other's lines by working arrangements or traffic facilities. 3. Agreement to divide the field. 4. Agreement to divide the earnings. 5. Agreement to divide the traffic. 6. Agreement to lease. 7. Agreement to consolidate. Each successive arrangement presents more chances of stability and permanence than its predecessor.

The first two methods have their home principally in England, although they are characteristic of all early attempts to avert competition. Not only do the railways agree as to the charges, but also as to the speed and accommodations. Contracts to run an equal number of trains at the same speed and with similar facilities are extremely common. For a long time reliance was placed on the existence of competition, but at present both railway officials and railway antagonists have definitely abandoned all faith in its efficacy.[1] Agreements as to rates, speed, and accommodation are to-day the well-nigh universal rule.

It is plain, however, that new agreements to maintain rates or afford facilities are difficult to enforce in the face of serious temptation to cut rates or underbid a rival company. The difficulty grows in proportion to the number of originally competitive lines. Hence in the United States, where the facility of constructing new competitive roads is practically unlimited, these methods, although often tried,[2] have proved ineffectual to prevent railway wars with the consequent abuses of fluctuations and injustice to the public. It was necessary to devise some other escape from competition.

The third method, that of division of the field, was naturally impracticable as long as any such plan might immediately be frustrated by the construction of a new line to invade the field. Some countries indeed, which foresaw the weakness of competition from the very outset, adopted this method, technically

---

[1] Report Select Committee on Railways (1882), Evid. qu. 2964 (Brown): "The days of competition are gone with railway companies." *Ibid.*, qu. 3896: "It cannot be to the interest of [the railways or] the public to carry on such competitive traffic, as they must either agree or stop ultimately." *Cf.* as to non-competition in accomodations, *etc.*, Joint Select Committee of 1872, Evid. (Farrer) qu. 7623, (Tyler) qu. 6893, 6914, (Wright) qu. 2548, (Scott) qu. 5384, *etc.*

[2] The arrangement made by the Saratoga conference of 1874 is the first example of such an agreement between the trunk lines. As to Western agreements between "honorable" roads at present, *cf.* Cullom Committee Rep., Test., p. 728.

called the principle of territorialization. Thus France parcelled out her territory among a small number of railways, principally radiating from Paris as a centre. The six "great companies" which control the transportation facilities are the direct product of the governmental policy. To use Mr. Chadwick's phrase, it is a system of competition *for* the field, not of competition *in* the field,[1] *i.e.* the stage of competition is removed to the period anterior to construction. In other words, the charters were granted to the highest bidders, to those companies which agreed to the conditions most favorable for the state. But this system proved defective in a double manner. In the first place, the rivalry between the corporations to obtain the coveted charters resulted in the assumption, by the successful competitors, of such unduly heavy burdens that after a short time they were confronted by the prospect of speedy ruin, until the state was compelled to interfere and lighten the burdens, thus abandoning the advantages that had been secured. In the second place, the almost absolute immunity from competition by new lines rendered the railways careless and averse to undertake improvements. While the French system, therefore, avoided in great measure railway wars and personal discriminations, it gave rise to serious complaints of extortionate charges and insufficient facilities — complaints which the recent agreements between the railways and the state are attempting to remedy.[2]

In those countries, however, where the original policy was that of unrestricted competition, the trend toward combination has also taken this form of territorialization. In England it is known as the districting system or district amalgamation, the chief examples being those of the North Eastern and Great Eastern railway companies.[3] The project has often been broached of enforcing a more systematic districting in the future; but the select committee of 1872 showed that such

---

[1] Chadwick, Results of different Principles of Legislation and Administration in Europe, *Journal of the Statistical Society*, vol. 22 (1859), pp. 381–420, esp. p. 385.

[2] Thoviste, Étude sur les conventions financières conclues entre l'État et les compagnies de chemins de fer (1886), pp. 121–124, 164–170.

[3] Joint Select Committee of 1872 on Railway Companies' Amalgamation, Evid. qu. 3660 *et seq.*

a plan was still impracticable, and enlarged on the inexpediency of conceding a full legal monopoly to the "districted" combinations.[1] In the United States there have been sporadic examples of the division of the field, where the separate parties to the combination agreed not to trench upon each other's territory; but the immense number of competitive lines has rendered arrangements of this kind for the most part illusory.

The next and most common step in the development of combination is the growth of the fourth and fifth forms — division of the traffic or the earnings. These are technically known as pools, — traffic pools and money pools,[2] — and it is against them that the fulminations of the Interstate Commerce law are directed. There is, perhaps, no single institution more commonly or more grievously misunderstood. For the odium that it has incurred the name itself is in part responsible. "Pooling" savors of a gambling transaction, of a wager or speculation; it immediately recalls to mind the "blind pools" of Wall Street notoriety, the accompaniments of games of chance. But railway pools are of an entirely different nature.[3] They are simply an attempt to escape the evils of an unrestricted competition while retaining all its essential advantages.

The first great benefit of all pooling machinery is a greater stability of charges. Continual and sudden fluctuations in rates are regarded by shippers as even worse than extortionate rates. Momentary and unexpected changes throw all business into confusion. Yet before the formation of pools these fluctuations were enormous. Let us take as an example the traffic between Chicago and New York, which received an immense impetus several years after the close of the war and the formation of the trunk lines. In 1869 the through tariffs from New York to Chicago changed twenty times during the year; in 1870, eleven times; in 1871, nine times; in 1875, five

[1] Report, pp. xl-xlii. *Cf.* Evid. (Farrer) qu. 7679, (Price) qu. 3815, *etc.*
[2] Or "cash" pools.
[3] *Cf.* in general, Cooley, Popular and Legal Aspects of Traffic-pooling (1884); Simon Sterne, Railroad Poolings and Discriminations (1879); Blanchard, Traffic Unity (1884); Pierson, The Passenger Pool (1884); Fink, The Railroad Problem and its Solution (1880).

times.[1] Not a year passed without frequent and often enormous fluctuations; *e.g.*, sudden changes from $1.88 to 40 cents per hundred and then back again. Yet after the formation of the trunk line pools of 1877-8, which were subsequently strengthened by the joint executive committee of 1879, there were for more than three and a half years *no* changes at all.[2] The manifest gain to the public in this increased steadiness of rates needs no further elucidation. Without the machinery devised for the Southern Railway and Steamship association in 1875 by Mr. Albert Fink, and extended by him to the trunk lines in 1877, this stability of rates would have been infinitely more difficult of accomplishment.

Secondly, not only do the pools succeed in obtaining a greater stability of the published tariffs, but they also tend to maintain actual charges to the level of the published tariffs by abating "rate-cutting," whether secret or open. It is conceded that personal discriminations or preferential rates form the chief abuse of our railway management. These special favors may indeed be cloaked under a variety of disguises, — such as underweighing or underbilling, Christmas gifts, and other arrangements whose exact tenor is known only to the freight manager and the individual shipper, — for the forms of personal preferences are limited only by the ingenuity of the railway officials. But secret rebates of this kind cannot be entirely prevented by any method, whether legal prohibition or voluntary agreement, as long as they remain secret. The sole remedy lies in absolute publicity and in removing as much as possible the temptation to cut rates. This the pooling system accomplishes with a fair degree of success, since the earnings of the railways are divided in fixed proportions irrespective of the traffic actually carried. The more effectual the pool and the more stringent the penalties

---

[1] Fink, Statistics regarding the Movement of Eastbound and Westbound Traffic over the Trunk Lines and connecting roads (1884), p. 39, comprising all changes from 1862 to 1884.

[2] From Feb. 15, 1878, to Aug. 6, 1881. Hudson, The Railways and the Public, p. 218, does not allude to these facts. His exposition is worse than inaccurate. It is so misleading as to be positively mischievous.

for infraction of the agreement, the greater the chances for maintenance of rates.

To object to pools because they have not completely attained their object — that of maintaining rates — is an argument of but little cogency. The most candid observers, even among those who at the outset opposed all forms of monopoly, admit that the situation has been materially improved since the existence of railway pools.[1] Such gross and palpable discriminations as those which built up the Standard Oil company would have been impossible under the late system of complete trunk line pools.[2] Preferential rates to-day in the district covered by the pooling systems are immeasurably less, both in number and extent, than ten years ago. The pressure exerted upon recalcitrant members is always stronger in a pool than in a mere agreement to maintain rates. If pools have not been entirely successful in preventing discriminations and railway wars, it is owing solely to lack of sufficiently coercive powers in the executive as well as to the fact that the pools are to a great extent beyond the law. The non-maintenance of rates is a violation of the pool, not a result of the pool. But if it be granted that pools do exert a beneficial influence in preventing preferential rates, then the surest method of augmenting this influence lies in strengthening the pools with their compulsory powers, not in abrogating them. The railway officials themselves have finally become conscious of this truth, and during the past few years we have had the singular spectacle of railway magnates demanding governmental interference with the railways in order to legalize, enforce, and regulate the pooling contracts. That such a step would be advantageous to the corporations is now substantially admitted; that it would be no less advantageous to the public is a fact which is only beginning to dawn on the public mind.[3]

[1] *Cf.* Simon Sterne, The Railway Question (1885), pp. 22–27, and in Cullom Report Test., pp. 71–77, as compared with his views in Report on the Internal Commerce of the United States (1879).

[2] United States Senate Committee on Labor and Education (1883), Test., vol. ii, p. 517.

[3] A fact obscured by such thoroughly partisan and unscientific works as that of Mr. Hudson.

The early pools were mainly "money pools." Thus the Chicago and Omaha pool of 1870 was based simply on the principle of a division of the total earnings after the deduction of a fixed percentage retained by each of the three roads as representing its expenses. But this arrangement was a manifest temptation to the individual lines to cut rates, increase the competitive business, and thus deduct a larger share to cover the increased expenses. Hence in 1874 the arrangement was modified so as to no longer allow deductions for expenses. The combination thus became, with a few minor exceptions, a "gross money" pool instead of a "net money" pool.[1] In the Southern Railway and Steamship association of 1875 the pooling policy was only one of the features of the combination, it being in other respects a forerunner of the "traffic associations," whose object is to facilitate the transaction of business, to provide proper means of amicably adjusting all differences, and to collectively and promptly enforce all agreements. Pools and traffic associations are of course entirely independent of each other; a pooling arrangement may be, and frequently is, one of the features of the traffic association, but there is no necessary connection between them. The one may and does exist without the other. In the association devised by Mr. Fink, with its elaborate machinery of executive officers, general commissioner, board of arbitration, *etc.*, the word pool is not mentioned at all. It was simply an attempt to substitute organized and harmonious action for the chaotic confusion and internecine rivalry between the southern railways.[2] Pooling arrangements were subsequently adopted, but only as a subordinate and entirely incidental feature of the general project. The contract provided for a net money pool, but with a comparatively small deduction for expenses.[3] The supplementary agreement of 1877 sought to increase the cohesiveness of the pool by providing for a penalty fund[4]

---

[1] Report on the Internal Commerce of the United States (1879).

[2] Proceedings of the Convention of the Southern Railway and Steamship Assoc. at Atlanta, Ga., Sept. 16, 17, 1875, pp. 11-17 (letter of Fink), 1-9 (agreement).

[3] Report on Internal Commerce of the United States (1876). Part II contains a reprint of the agreements.

[4] 20 per cent of the amount received on all joint business transacted.

deposited by each road with the commissioner as a pledge of good faith, and forfeitable upon proven infraction of the agreement.

When the Westbound Trunk Line pool was formed by Mr. Fink in 1877 after a protracted and desperate war. the policy of dividing the business instead of the earnings was carried into effect. It was a "traffic pool" instead of a money pool, and was further developed in the joint executive agreement of 1879. The joint agent was invested with the duty of making the weekly accounts and of specifying the roads which had carried less than their agreed percentage ; and such roads were bound to promptly restore the balance by removing from the other companies their excess.[1] This was known as the "equalizing of freight" or "diversion of traffic." In the new agreement of 1882 the payment of money balances or settlements in net earnings was introduced, and for two years no transfers of tonnage were made.[2] But to some extent the practice re-appeared, and caused so much dissatisfaction among the shippers that in the agreement of 1885 it was definitely discarded and provision made for the prompt payment of money balances by preliminary deposits to the credit of certain trustees.[3] Since October, 1884, settlements moreover were made in gross, not net earnings. In the division of the eastbound dead freight and live stock traffic, as well as among the other associations throughout the country, this method of settlement had become the general rule. So accurately were the percentages allotted, that the amount of money balances was phenomenally small, in some cases amounting to less than one per mill of the gross revenue.[4] This is a fact commonly overlooked, but which reflects the greatest possible credit on the organizers of the traffic arrangements.

---

[1] *Cf.* the contract in Hepburn Committee Report, Exhibits, p. 63.

[2] *Cf.* statistics in Fink, Letter in relation to the Diversion of Freight, Exhibit No. 3, Third Report of Board of Railroad Commissioners of New York (1885), p. 120.

[3] Contract between the trunk lines, Nov. 6, 1885, arts. x–xiii ; reprinted in Cullom Com. Rep., App., pp. 237–244.

[4] In the Southern Railway and Steamship Association from 1876 to 1886, gross earnings were $82,000,000 ; total money balances, $461,295, or 0.56 per cent. The

The idea that pools are a product of American ingenuity is most erroneous. The present form of railway federation or traffic association is indeed peculiar to America, and represents the life-long work of Albert Fink, but the pooling arrangements are only ancillary features. Pools are not new. Europe learned the futility and inexpediency of opposing pools many years ago. They have been found to be the surest means of preventing unjust discriminations. In England they are known as "joint purse" arrangements, and generally take the form of money pools because of the greater consolidation of the lines. Agreements to charge equal rates for competitive traffic have been much more uniformly observed in Great Britain than with us, and hence the more advanced arrangements for the division of traffic have not been so necessary.

following interesting figures relative to the trunk lines have never been published, but rest on official authority, and have been inspected by me. The details for each road are for obvious reasons omitted.

	TONNAGE CARRIED.	GROSS REVENUE.	REVENUE BALANCES.	PER CENT.
Westbound, 1877 to 1886 ..	8,984,294	$36,356,163	$482,537	1.32
Eastbound, 1882 to 1885...	30,423,749	65,133,997	272,015	0.41
Boston and New England, Live Stock, 1882 to 1886 .	1,347,407	3,377,487	23,072	0.68
All divisions, 1877 to 1886 .	49,792,626	129,530,377	1,200,729	0.9

I add a few examples, without mentioning the exact date or species of traffic:

RAILROAD.	TOTAL RECEIPTS.	BALANCES.	PER CENT.
Baltimore and Ohio	$91,133	$105 rec'd	0.1
New York Central and Hudson River ...	3,861,364	612 paid	0.016
Pennsylvania	18,350,020	47,657 paid	0.25

The balances paid by the different companies which carried in excess of their allotments were on the total traffic:

New York Central . . . . $\frac{14}{100}$ of 1 cent per 100 pounds.
Pennsylvania . . . . $\frac{23}{100}$ " " " "
Grand Trunk . . . . $\frac{11}{100}$ " " " "
Lackawanna . . . . $\frac{10}{100}$ " " " "

But joint purse agreements are not at all uncommon.[1] Many of them have been made under the express sanction of Parliament or the commission to which the power of approval has been delegated. The apportionments of traffic are moreover made for much longer periods than in the United States, — a fact ascribable to the comparative constancy of business and the settled character of commercial relations. Thus Gladstone allotted pooling percentages for a term of five years in 1851 and made a further award for fourteen years in 1857.[2] In 1853 the manager of a single railway called attention to twenty-seven such pooling arrangements made by his own line within a very limited period, dividing the traffic in all salient points. The railways among themselves and the railways and canals are shown to form a "happy family."[3] It is simply an additional proof of Gladstone's statement that competition between railways is like a lovers' quarrel : *breves inimicitiae, amicitiae sempiternae*.[4] The joint fund arrangements are found in large numbers to-day, and the clearing house acts as the agent of the interested parties, in this respect very much like the general commissioners of our traffic associations.[5] In England, while Parliament may still disclose a certain jealousy of the working arrangements of this kind, it does not think of pro-

---

[1] As an example at present *cf.* the lines at Preston, Select Com. (1881), qu. 12,050.

[2] The first pool was between the Great Northern, the London and North Western, and the Midland railways; the second between the same and the Manchester, Sheffield and Lincolnshire. Parliament has sanctioned pools between the South Eastern and the London, Chatham and Dover railways; and also between the London, Brighton and South Coast and the South Eastern companies.

[3] Rep. Sel. Com. on Railway and Canal Bills (1853), Evid. (Huish) qu. 120-310.

[4] Speech on bill of 1844 (Hansard, vol. 76, pp. 480-509). Gladstone adds: "I would no more trust the railway proprietors on railway matters than I would Gracchus speaking of sedition. I know of nothing more chilling than the hope which railway directors hold out from competition." The whole speech may be found in full in Galt, Railway Reform, its importance and practicability considered (1864), App 254-266. Galt's book itself is a highly fanciful plea for uniform cheap charges, based on Rowland Hill's postal reform. The first edition was published in 1843, and demands state purchase.

[5] Rep. Joint Select Committee on Railway Companies' Amalgamation (1872). Evid. (Dawson) qu. 5571-2. The clearing house does not fix the percentages as did our pool commissioners.

hibiting them; it simply makes them subject to governmental regulation. The wisest thinkers, even among those who cannot be deemed by any means apologists of the railways, confess that some of the present abuses may be obviated by a more intimate fusion of interests in this direction.[1]

On the continent pooling arrangements are carried out to a much greater extent, and personal discriminations are hence correspondingly less frequent. In Germany they are known as *Kartellen* or *Instradirungs-verträge*.[2] Owing to the greater complexity of the lines and the lesser degree of consolidation, they generally take the form of traffic pools. One important example of a money pool was the great German Austrian union (*Deutsch-oesterreichischer Verband*), an international association from 1868 to 1873. But this was finally abandoned on account of the difficulty of making the exact allotments, it being not a gross money pool as in England or with us, but a net money pool with deduction for expenses.[3] Since the railways have been almost entirely purchased by the state in Prussia, the necessity for pools has diminished, but the rivalry between the various state systems is so intense that a series of interstate pools has sprung up. In order to facilitate the execution of these agreements it has even been provided that the shipper shall no longer have the right to select the route by which his goods are to be transported.[4] The railways ship the goods as they please, the sole condition being that the freight is to be carried by the cheapest or otherwise most favorable line. Not only are the pools effectually enforced between the state railways themselves but also,

---

[1] Sir B. Samuelson, Report on Railway Goods Tariffs (1886), p. 22. That the railway men favor this plan is of course obvious; *cf.* Grierson, Railway Rates (1886), sec. xvi.

[2] Or Instradirungs-vereinbarungen.

[3] Reitzenstein, Ueber einige Verwaltungseinrichtungen und das Tarifwesen auf den Eisenbahnen Englands, pp. 152 *et seq.* This contains a comparison of the English and German pools. For other cases, see Ulrich, Das Eisenbahntarifwesen, § 63.

[4] The sole exception is in case of goods subject to customs duties; Beschluss des Bundesraths, March 12, 1885, which changes § 50 of the Betriebsreglement. *Cf.* also Endemann, Das Recht der Eisenbahnen (1886), Fünfter Abschnitt.

when there is any danger of serious competition, between the railways and the waterways, including both canal and river traffic. In the allotment of percentage, moreover, the shortest line is not taken as the basis, but the shorter road is deemed equal to the longer road only up to twenty per cent of the longer distance.[1] The pooling arrangements in Germany have been of signal service in simplifying and equalizing the charges, which prior to their introduction were of the most complicated and often outrageously unjust character; and to-day they still perform the most valuable services in international traffic. No one any longer thinks of opposing them in principle.[2]

In Austria, where the state and private railways exist side by side, money and traffic pools are of daily occurrence. No sooner is a new route opened than it receives its share of the competitive traffic, and is thus deprived of any pretext to undertake a railway war. It may be declared that all competitive traffic in Austria is strictly pooled.[3] The state railways themselves divide earnings or traffic with the water routes, and are thus able to avoid crying discriminations. In Belgium, where one large private company, the *Grand Central Belge*, has been the most formidable potential competitor of the state railways, the government has concluded a pooling agreement for the strict division of all competitive traffic. The line over which the shipment is made receives all the *frais fixes*, or terminal charges, as well as one-half of the *frais variables*, or movement charges. The remainder is pooled in fixed percentages.[4] The sad experience of railway wars and exorbitant

[1] This is known as the doctrine of "virtual" or "computed" distances. Schreiber, Das Tarifwesen der Eisenbahnen, S. 245–249. It is somewhat similar to our "constructive mileage."

[2] *Cf.* von der Leyen, Die nordamerikanischen Eisenbahnen (1885), S. 296: "The European expert finds these arrangements entirely unobjectionable" ("findet in solchen Verbänden nichts Verwerfliches"). *Cf.* also Obermayer, Ueber Tarifverbände und Eisenbahnkartelle (1879).

[3] Sax, Die Verkehrsmittel, Bd. II, S. 102. For full details as to a late instance (the Arlberg line), see *The Railroad Gazette*, 1884, p. 636.

[4] According to the doctrine of "virtual distances." But if the longer line's mileage exceeds the other by more than 25 per cent, it receives nothing beyond the terminals and one-half of the movement charges.

discriminations in the past has long since convinced the government of the absolute necessity of some agreements with its private competitors. Just as competition in general pulls the best men down to the level of the most unscrupulous, so in the competition between the state and the private railways the government itself was compelled to descend to the methods of private companies and practise discriminations of the most flagrant nature, in some cases going so far as to discriminate against its own property in the shape of canals. Until the state owns all the railways, such pools will be necessary and beneficial to all parties concerned.

In France the principle of territorialization from the very outset has materially lessened the need of pooling arrangements. If the division of the field were absolute, the division of traffic or earnings could not exist, for the same result would be attained in either way. In some few cases, however, the chief lines partially overlap each other and thus give rise to competitive centres, but the dangers of competition are immediately obviated by the formation of pools, which are recognized as perfectly legitimate.[1] The state line itself has made such a compact with the Orleans company, in which the percentages depend to a certain extent on the differences of grade.[2] France has no faith in railway competition. In Italy the railways are sharply divided into two networks, and there is no competition and hence no necessity for pools. All international traffic, however, is effectively pooled. In Holland, where the pooling policy is far less developed, the results of the competition between the railways, and especially the railways and waterways, have been so unsatisfactory and the discriminations so crying that the parliamentary commission of 1881-2 desired to seek refuge from the railway wars in universal consolidation, and would have advocated state purchase had it not

---

[1] A prominent French official writes to me as to the existence of money pools between railways, and even between railways and canals: "Il en existe plusieurs exemples. C'est chose parfaitement admise." So, *e.g.*, the Chemins de fer d'Ouest et d'Orleans.

[2] Convention de 1883 avec la Compagnie d'Orleans, art. 16, in Picard, Chemins de fer français, t. 6 (1885), p. 396.

been for financial difficulties. Mere legislative prohibition of discriminations they confessed to be futile, and therefore proposed to hasten on the process of combination by furthering the consolidation of certain smaller lines, and by refusing charters to any new competing lines.[1]

All the European countries, therefore, inculcate the same lesson. Unjust discriminations and especially preferential rates are found in inverse ratio to the pools. Where the pools are legalized and most effective, as in Germany and Belgium, the abuses are least; where the pools are less frequent, as in England, the abuses are greater; where the pools are rare and ineffective, as in Holland, the abuses are scandalous. Experience is no less convincing than theory. As long as there is no complete consolidation we cannot prevent both pools and discriminations. We must choose between them. The full development of the one means the disappearance of the other. With an universal pool, we can stop all unjust discriminations produced by the stress of competition; with partial pools we can *pro tanto* abate the discriminations. Nothing will be gained by the attempt to stop pools. We may prohibit them, but cannot prevent them. And if they could be prevented, they would simply disappear for a time; the causes which rendered their existence necessary would reassert themselves, and in the long run prove invincible, with the only result that in the mean time the country would have been exposed to an intensification of the very evils which it was desired to suppress.

That there is a possible danger in pools is indeed not to be denied. The inference, however, is simply the necessity of effective public regulation. What the public fears is the temptation to impose exorbitant charges. The policy of avoiding competition from the outset on the continent of Europe has certainly had some influence in preventing so quick a reduction of charges as with us. But rates in this country are perhaps as low as can be reasonably desired.

[1] *Cf.* the report itself (October, 1882). For an abstract, see *Archiv für Eisenbahnwesen*, 1883, S. 587–590. *Cf.* Jacqmin, Chemins de fer des Pays-bas, 2me éd., p. 87.

There is no serious complaint of extortion, and there is far less probability of extortionate charges here than in European countries, because of the exceptionally large amount of water competition in the United States. The gravamen of the complaints is discrimination, not extortion. There is no need of conjuring up phantom dangers. We are actually confronted by certain specific abuses, and it is a superficial policy to abolish the means of preventing these abuses because of the dim possibility of other abuses which do not exist.

One misconception more fatal than any yet discussed still remains. It is commonly supposed that pooling entirely prevents competition. This is a mistake. Pooling maintains the advantages of a healthy competition and at the same time prevents the dangers of an utterly unrestricted or "cut-throat" competition. The mere agreement to divide traffic or earnings in certain percentages does not put a stop to all competition. Each of the various roads will still attempt to procure as much business as can possibly be obtained in a fair and open manner. If any line while maintaining the published rates is yet enabled to run above its allotted percentage, this surplus will justify the railway in demanding an increased percentage in the new allotment that is to be made at the expiration of the monthly or yearly pooling arrangement. The incentive to fair and healthy competition is not removed; each line will endeavor to vie with its rival in accommodations and facilities. But the temptation to take unfair advantages of its rivals is diminished, for an increase of traffic due to rebates or violations of the pooling agreement manifestly cannot justify a claim for increased percentages. A successful pool prevents railway wars with the accompanying discriminations, but does not prevent healthy emulation to attract business. It simply raises the plane of competition to a higher level.[1]

The abolition of pooling would in fact hasten the very result which it is desired to avoid. Division of the traffic and the earnings form, as we have seen, the fourth and fifth step in the

[1] This is another of the points entirely overlooked by Hudson, The Railways and the Republic, p. 229.

progress of combination. The final steps are lease and absolute consolidation. The tendency to combination is irresistible; all endeavors to stem the current have been and will be futile.[1] If therefore pools, which still permit competition to a limited degree, be abolished, the process of complete consolidation, which utterly precludes competition, will be accelerated. Under the system of division of earnings, the weaker roads are still enabled to procure a share of the business and thus maintain a limited competition; remove the guarantee of allotted percentages, and it is simply a question of time before the weaker roads are driven to the wall and then bought out by their more sturdy competitors. No clause in the Interstate Commerce act prohibits the stronger line from lowering its charges and thus inaugurating a war of rates, provided it be done publicly. The enforced publicity of charges is undoubtedly an immense step in advance; but while no increase of charges can be made until after ten days' public notice, reductions in the charges may take place without previous public notice.[2] Railway wars are hence by no means prevented. Pools are indeed a makeshift, but the disappearance of this modified and partial form of combination would most assuredly lead to a more complete and absolute form of combination. The logical outcome will be a concentration of the railways in the hands of an exceedingly small number of corporations, and the development may even be carried to a stage which the telegraph lines have already reached — a practical monopoly of one huge corporation. The federal law is thus unwittingly hastening the very result which it intended to frustrate. It defeats the very purpose which it was designed to accomplish. Our legislators imagined that

---

[1] *Cf.* English Select Committee (1872), p. xxvi: "While it is extremely doubtful to what extent the less complete forms of combination admit of competition, and what is the value of such competition, there can be little doubt, judging from the past, that they cannot be maintained as the ultimate forms, and are sure, whatever principles may be laid down by committees or commissions, to end in complete fusion. So much stronger is the power of wealth, self-interest, and united action on the part of the companies, acting each in its own case with clearness and decision, than that of any general principles by which committees and commissions have supposed that the public interest might be protected."

[2] Sec. 6 of act.

they could prevent combination by prohibiting pooling; in reality they have destroyed that which still preserves partial competition and by prohibiting pools have made ultimate consolidation less remote. In their anxiety to prevent monopoly they have taken the surest step to create monopoly; in their ignorance of economic laws, while hoping to raise an impassable barrier to combination they have in reality levelled the course. The result will be the exact opposite of their anticipations.

The progress of this consolidation may indeed be arrested for a time. Railway wars cannot of course be the normal condition, and the short-haul clause of the law will have some slight effect in preventing the inordinately low war-rates to centres of competition. It is therefore possible, nay, almost certain, that the results of the pooling policy will be attained in another way — through the medium of "differentials." Rather than enter upon a war of rates, the stronger roads, which through their better facilities would tend to carry the larger portion of the traffic, will consent to give the weaker lines a "differential," *i.e.*, allow them to charge so much less per ton, and to attract in consequence more business. The limit of the "differential"[1] will depend naturally on the desire or ability of the weaker line to declare war rather than to accept less than the demanded differential. This system, however, is virtually, although not nominally, tantamount to pooling, in so far as it is a form of combination which still retains a certain amount of competition. But if successful, it is open to the same objections as pooling; while the absence of any vigorous executive authority to enforce the agreements will be felt still more strongly than has hitherto been the case in the traffic associations and pools. This policy of what we may call "differential pools" cannot possibly be stopped by any law.

The anti-pooling clause[2] of the federal law thus sins in

[1] This technical phrase is used in an entirely different manner from that described in my first essay, POLITICAL SCIENCE QUARTERLY, June, 1887, pp. 236, 237.

[2] Sec. 5: "That it shall be unlawful for any common carrier . . . to enter into any contract, agreement, or combination with any other common carrier or carriers, for the pooling of freights of different and competing railroads, or to divide between them the aggregate or net proceeds of the earnings of such railroads, or any portions thereof."

a double manner. It weakens the government in its attempt to prevent discriminations, and it is destined to produce a state of affairs precisely the contrary of what was intended. The first three sections of the act, which define and forbid unjust discriminations,[1] are in effect simply declarative of the common law, although based almost literally on Cardwell's Traffic act of 1854. It may well be doubted whether this mere legislative enunciation and prohibition will suffice to abolish the evils complained of. The definition is so utterly vague as to be susceptible of varied interpretations; and whatever interpretation be adopted, it must, as we have shown in the previous essay, be so essentially elastic as to preclude any hard and fast application. Whether the prohibition of unjust discrimination will be anything more than the expression of a pious wish, depends largely on the commission; but the law imposes on the commission an unnecessarily severe burden, and by prohibiting pools removes what would have been a most serviceable crutch with which the better to support the burden. If self-help, or at least private co-operation, be a fundamental feature of the American polity, then this law violates the American idea, for it voluntarily resigns the advantages that would accrue from the self-help of the railways. I do not object to state interference, but I do object to the hasty abandonment of an institution which tends to decrease the necessity of state interference. And when the abolition of the institution results, as is assuredly the case with pools, in hastening the advent of the very monopoly which it was designed to avoid, then the prohibition becomes not only unwise but absolutely absurd. The anti-pooling clause is a sad

---

[1] Sec. 1 declares that "all charges . . . shall be reasonable and just; and every unjust and unreasonable charge . . . is prohibited and declared to be unlawful." Sec. 2 defines an unjust discrimination as the charging any persons different amounts for a "like and contemporaneous service in the transportation of a like kind of traffic under substantially similar circumstances and conditions." Sec. 3 declares it unlawful "to make or give any undue or unreasonable preference or advantage to any particular person, company, firm, corporation, or locality, or any particular description of traffic, in any respect whatsoever, or to subject any particular person, company, firm, corporation, or locality, or any particular description of traffic to any undue or unreasonable prejudice or disadvantage in any respect whatsoever." These three clauses are virtual repetitions, and afford no basis for a definite decision.

evidence of the results of demagogic ignorance in producing hasty and ill-advised legislation. The Philistines of the daily press exaggerate the dangers of the short-haul section, because these lie on the surface; but for the far more important fifth section of the federal law they have neither eye nor ear. Fortunately pooling will practically continue in another form which Congress will be powerless to prevent.

The Senate select committee of 1886 has at least this claim to respectful attention, that it opposed the prohibition of pools. The abandonment of its position was an inexcusable concession to popular clamor. A careful analysis of the testimony discloses the fact that not only all the railway officials, but also a large majority of the intelligent shippers, had become convinced of the break-down of competition and the necessity of pooling. The railway men opposed unrestricted competition because it curtailed profits; the intelligent shippers opposed competition because it produced discrimination.[1] Both were correct. The Senate committee therefore, swayed by the unanimous opinion of the railway men and the preponderant weight of testimony on the part of the public, decided that "the evils to be attributed to pooling are not those which most need correction," and that "it would seem wiser to permit such agreements rather than by prohibiting them ... to endanger the success of the methods of regulation proposed for the prevention of unjust discrimination."[2] That the members of the committee, with a few honorable exceptions, should have seen fit to abdicate their strong position is sincerely to be regretted. The clause as it stands is in defiance of the teachings of experience and the laws of political economy.[3]

---

[1] Among the shippers who uphold pooling may be mentioned (*vid.* Report, Testimony) Bacon (707), Burrows (1170), Chapin (684), Dunnell (1330), Elliott (695), Field (655), Francis (919), Goodman (1104), Gue (1070), Herrick (217), Joseph (1030), Lowry (721), Meek (1012), Miller (269), Murch (941), Noble (988), Phelps (1410), Reynolds (1185), Root (1198), Speare (347), Tredway (841), Welch (1445), Wicke (766), and Williams (1059). The number of shippers who oppose pools is far smaller, and of these the great majority base their opposition on their belief in "free, open competition in railways, as in other things"!

[2] Report, p. 201.

[3] Even European experts who are by no means admirers of the American rail-

Free competition between railways, as a regulator of transportation charges, is thus a mere chimera.[1] But "competition" has become such a shibboleth with a certain class of reformers that it may be well to devote a few words to other forms which are advocated as panaceas for existing abuses.

Perhaps the most common recommendation is that of *competition of carriers on the line.* Divorce entirely the business of the common carrier from that of the highway; let the corporation indeed own the rail*way*, but let every one have the right to run his own trains and use his own locomotives on this railway. This indeed would be perfect competition, but of a very different kind from the competition *between* the railways that we have been considering. Alluring as is this plan at first blush, it is open to three vital objections. 1. It is impracticable, or, if practicable, would be far more costly. 2. It would not cure the great evils of the present system. 3. It would produce abuses far worse than any which now exist.

First, the plan is impracticable, or, if practicable, would be far more costly. The project is not new. Competition between carriers was the original theory. The early railway acts were based on the canal and turnpike acts. When the system of turnpike trusts was inaugurated in England in 1706,[2] the original public character of the king's highway disappeared, and the control fell into semi-private hands. But the highway of course remained free to all on payment of the tolls. With the advent of canals the private speculative element was introduced into transportation; for although a very few of the canals were put into the hands of canal trusts, the first canal[3] and most of the others were built by private individuals and corporations. The early canal acts, however, invariably contained the clause

way system concur in this opinion. See *Archiv für Eisenbahnwesen,* 1887, S. 333. *Cf.* also Jeans, Railway Problems (1887), p. 518.

[1] *Cf.* Bontoux, Die Concurrenz im Eisenbahnwesen (1873).

[2] The old Watling road. The first turnpike act empowering the raising of tolls was passed 1663, but the power was given to overseers, not trusts. It is only in the last few decades that the turnpike trusts are giving way to the highway boards and that the public character is being restored.

[3] Duke of Bridgewater's canal from Liverpool to Manchester. Acts of 1758, 1759, and 1762.

that all persons without distinction should have free liberty to use the canal on payment of tolls. When the first tramway bill was enacted in 1801,[1] it adopted this idea, and provided, among other sections borrowed *verbatim* from the canal acts, that all persons should have the right to use the tramway with their own horses and wagons. In the charter of the first railway built with the avowed purpose of using steam locomotives a similar clause was introduced, modified so as to meet the exigencies of the new methods of transportation.[2] For many years the identical provision is found in all the railway acts.

In the United States analogous provisions were inserted in the early charters. So, *e.g.*, in the charter of the Ithaca and Oswego railroad.[3] In the general railroad law of Prussia competition between the carriers is likewise legalized, after the expiration of three years from the opening of the railway.[4] In France the principle was carried so far as actually to distinguish between the charge for the use of the track, or the toll (*droit de péage*), and the charge for the transportation itself (*prix de transport*). To this day even, the concessions of the railways contain the legal distinction.[5] Everywhere, in fact, a sharp line was drawn between the two functions of the railway company — that of providing the public highway free to all and that of furnishing the means of transportation on the highway. The railway company was not excluded from the latter function, but it was thought that its activity in this direction would be very slight.

The experience of a very few years totally destroyed all these

[1] The Surrey railway from Wordsworth to Croydon. *Cf.* Francis, History of the English Railway (1851), vol. i.

[2] Liverpool and Manchester Railway act, 7 Geo. IV, cap. 49, cl. 165: "All persons shall have free liberty to use with carriages all roads, ways, and passages for the purpose of conveying goods or passengers or cattle."

[3] Sec. 12: "All persons paying the toll aforesaid may, with suitable and proper carriages, use and travel upon the said railroad, subject to such rules and regulations as the said corporators are authorized to make by the ninth section of this act. Laws of New York, 1828, p. 17. The "proper carriages" of course included the steam-carriages.

[4] Eisenbahngesetz, 1838, § 27.

[5] Picard, Chemins de fer français, t. v, p. 184; Jacqmin, De l'exploitation des chemins de fer, t. i, p. 20.

anticipations. As a matter of fact the transportation was conducted solely by the railway company. Even in those countries which earnestly endeavored to enforce the provisions, legislation was impotent to check the natural tendency. There were weighty reasons which did and always must militate against the success of any such scheme.

The most obvious objection, of course, is the technical one. The technical character of the railway undertaking renders it imperative to have unity of administration. If every shipper could run his own trains, it would be almost impossible to preserve order or avoid serious accidents. The private trains would have no means of enjoying terminal or other conveniences, and if the railway company were compelled to afford these conveniences, it would soon display such power of annoying the private shippers as to render the plan nugatory. At a time when the engineers were grappling with the problem and devising schemes for allowing two trains to pass each other on a single track, the project of competition between private locomotives might be plausible; to-day it is unintelligible and absurd. Entirely apart, moreover, from the objection of technical impracticability, is the vital difficulty of increased expense. The cost of service would be so enormously increased as to result in higher, not in lower, charges. All shippers would not be large shippers. The number of those who could despatch a train with forty cars would be exceedingly limited. The result would be the necessity of ten engines for small trains where one now suffices, as well as a vast increase in the extent and facilities of the terminals and a proportionate increase in operating expenses. The control of transportation is indissolubly bound up with the control of the roadbed.

But secondly, the scheme would not cure the great evils of the present system. What is sought is the abolition of unjust discrimination. It is difficult to see how free competition of the carriers would effect this. The railway would still be empowered to charge tolls, but it is impossible, as has been shown in the preceding essay, that these tolls should be alike for all classes or distances. The expenses of the private trains would of course be proportional to cost of service; the cheap goods would be more expensive to transport than the dear goods. In order, therefore, to render the transportation of cheap or distant articles at all possible, the tolls would have to vary in a large degree in their favor.[1] According to the principle of value of service it would be requisite to have classification and local discrimination in tolls, as in the turnpike and canal tolls, but in a necessarily increased proportion. The private shippers of coal, *e.g.*, would have to defray not only the operating expenses proper but also the fixed charges representing the capital invested in the rolling stock; the railway company, on the other hand, could afford to transport this coal at lower rates, because it could compensate by charging higher rates on other traffic which is better able to pay. Under a *régime* of competition of carriers, therefore, it will be necessary to differentiate the tolls correspondingly unless the present traffic in cheap or distant goods is to be entirely stopped. The discriminations represented by the tolls would be precisely equal to the present discriminations in the total rates. To fix the tolls by law would not mend matters, for if the law can successfully fix tolls, it can equally well fix the total charges as imposed at present. The principle involved is the same. But if the extent of tolls is left to the discretion of the railway companies, then the condition of affairs is not improved a whit. The difficulties of regulation according to a well-digested system would not be diminished.

But thirdly, it is very probable that abuses would be engendered far worse than any which exist. There would be such an evident gain in the larger shippers combining to lessen running expenses that before long competition would again forcedly result in combination. This would practically intensify personal discriminations. The large shippers might through combination reduce the charges to a minimum, and, not being common carriers, would refuse to take the goods of the smaller shippers. The latter would thus be put at an immense disad-

---

[1] Mr. Hudson proposes equal mileage tolls (Railways and the Republic, p. 397). But the impracticability and inadvisability of this have already been shown.

vantage, while now they have at least an equal right to insist on transportation. If it be objected that the small shippers might also combine, the answer is that the practical difficulties in the way would be well-nigh insuperable; and that even if they were overcome we should no longer have the condition of free competition between the carriers. The very basis of the argument would fall away.

The legitimacy of such a conclusion is emphasized by the history of the English railways. For there, as in other countries, we find vestiges of an arrangement which is only a slight variation of the scheme proposed. That is, although we do not find cases of competition between carriers who own their locomotives, there have been instances of competition between shippers who own their own cars. This is technically known as the principle of *separation of traction and carrier*.[1] The most striking example of the inadequacy of the remedy suggested is seen in the case of the coal companies. Each of these as a rule owned its own cars. Yet the result of the competition has been the building up of a few gigantic monopolies to the exclusion of the smaller shippers. The agglomerated companies always succeeded in procuring better facilities in the way of storage of coal, *etc.*, in the depots than the isolated small shippers, and the inevitable tendency has reasserted itself. So far has this process been carried as to practically preclude small shippers from sending coal without the consent of the larger companies.[2] Separation between motor and carrier would aggravate, not diminish, the abuses.

So incisive are the arguments against free competition of carriers that every careful scientific investigation of the question has abundantly proved the fruitlessness of the scheme. Already in 1839 an English committee reported, after an extensive review of the facts, that such a plan was no less undesirable than impracticable.[3] In 1844 Gladstone's committee repeated the

[1] Or of " motor " and carrier.
[2] *Cf.* Royal Commission (1866), Evid. qu. 12,502–12,519; *ibid.* (1865), qu. 9772 *et seq.*, 9853 *et seq.* Already in 1853 we find the same tendency. *Cf.* Joint Select Committee (1853), Fifth Report, pp. 201–206.
[3] Select Committee on Railways (1839), Second Report.

elaborate refutation.[1] But the attempt to enforce this competition was nevertheless found in the charters. Cardwell's committee of 1853 still discussed the project.[2] But from that time the clauses in the charter were regarded as mere archaic curiosities. The Duke of Devonshire's commission abandoned the fiction once and for all.[3] In Chichester Fortescue's committee the efforts of the early legislation are reviewed with a grim sarcasm;[4] and, finally, in Mr. Ashley's recent committee the whole matter is not even deemed worthy of separate mention.[5]

But although England had been radically cured of her early misconceptions, ignorance of English experience led to a revamping of the old doctrines on the continent. The matter was taken up at the close of the sixties in Germany, and for several years would-be reformers and even economic congresses sounded the praises of the new panacea.[6] It became, as has been wittily remarked, the *enfant terrible* of the railway question in Germany and Austria. Thrown out of one window, it came bobbing in at the next.[7] Book after book was written to explain the advantages of the system, but science and commonsense again triumphed,[8] and to-day the project is considered as definitely laid to rest. Yet scarcely has the matter been finally decided on the continent when we are called upon to go over the same tedious ground in the United States. Here too the plan is elaborately set forth[9] with a naive confidence in its

[1] Select Committee (1844), p. 19, Appendix to Evidence.

[2] Joint Select Committee (1853), Fifth Report, p. 8: "In theory the railway is like a common highway; in practice, no one can carry upon a railway but the owners of the line."

[3] Royal Commission (1867), Report, § 7.

[4] "Committees and commissioners, carefully chosen, have for the last thirty years clung to one form of competition after another," *etc.* Select Committee (1873), Report, p. xviii.

[5] Select Committee on Railways (Rates and Fares), 1882.

[6] Technically known as "Die Freiheit der Schiene."

[7] Sax, Die Verkehrsmittel, Bd. II, S. 112.

[8] *Cf.* the discussions in Reitzenstein, Die Gütertarife der Eisenbahnen (1874), S. 42-59; Perrot, Die Eisenbahnreform (1871), S. 34-47; G. Cohn, Streitfragen der Eisenbahnpolitik (1874), S. 17-32: Bilinski, Die Eisenbahntarife (1875), S. 14 *et seq.*

[9] Hudson, The Railways and the Republic (1886), ch. x, esp. p. 400. Mr. Hudson is just about twenty years behind the times. His arguments are almost word for word those of Dorn, Aufgaben der Eisenbahnpolitik (1874).

novelty and efficacy — a confidence that can be excused only on the assumption of woful ignorance of the literature or absolute incapacity to learn from experience. But it plainly cannot be the duty of a scientist to refute in detail what has been disproved time and time again. The practical character of the American public, moreover, is so well assured as to render the necessity of any such refutation extremely improbable.

Another variation of this form of competition deserves a passing notice, *viz.*, the demand for the enforcement of *running powers*. This theory is supposed to uphold competition by allowing the trains of any one railway to pass over the tracks of the other. The English Parliament, after having abandoned all the other theories of competition, still clung to this; and one of the main features of Cardwell's act of 1854 was an attempt to realize this idea. In the United States also it is advanced as a panacea. But Robert Stephenson already in 1853 emphatically condemned such running powers as incompatible with safety and practical administration.[1] The committee of 1872 finally forsook the old position and came to the conclusion that in *all* cases where running powers existed they were the result of voluntary agreements.[2] It is practically impossible to compel the railways to grant such powers against their will, and if it were possible it would not be wise.[3] It would be far more expensive and dangerous, and it would put a check to all railway building by powerful capitalists, for it would render the quantity of traffic carried by any one line absolutely uncertain and subject to the discretion of the government. In France, likewise, there have been repeated attempts to enforce these running powers, but the only case in which they have not ignominiously failed has been that of branch, not competing, lines.[4]

[1] Select Committee on Railway and Canal Bills (1853), Evid., pp. 115, 116.
[2] Select Committee on Railway Cos. Amalgamation (1872), Rep., pp. xlv, xlvi.
[3] Hudson, Railways and the Republic, p. 382, gives a few familiar examples of one track being used jointly by two railways. But that is quite another thing from allowing one track to be used by *all* the other lines, especially if the first one does not consent. *Voluntary* arrangements are not enforceable running *powers*.
[4] Thus in the revision of the *cahiers de charge* imposed on all the "great companies" in 1857-59 these running powers were reserved to all branch lines and prolongations on payment of a fixed *droit de péage*. *Cf.* the documents themselves, titre vi,

But the most amusing error remains to be noticed. Running powers or "working arrangements" when voluntary are just the opposite of what they are supposed to be. In lieu of being a form of competition, they are a form of combination — the forerunner of pools and frequently their concomitant. The railways agree to forward traffic over each other's lines, or to divide the traffic in cases where they use the same line, not in order to maintain competition but in order to avoid competition. And if enforceable running powers were universal, they would simply result again in private agreements. It would not be an advance of competition but a check to competition. Even if it were practicable, it would simply accelerate the process which it was designed to arrest. Compulsory competition is an absurdity. Fortunately the Interstate Commerce law expressly disclaims all intention of enforcing such working arrangements,[1] although it may well be doubted whether the legislators were actuated by the reasons just recounted. The prohibition of pools militates against the acceptance of any such flattering imputation.

There remains finally the subject of *water competition*. In so far as we have to deal with artificial waterways the same unmistakable tendency to combination is apparent. The competition of canals is virtually of no importance as the regulator of railway charges. In the first quarter of this century the charges on the English canals were so extortionate and the abuses so extravagant that great hopes were staked on the competition of the railways. The railways indeed did compete with the canals, but so effectually as to silence all competition. They bought up the canals or amalgamated with them, and before long the condition of affairs was reversed. New canals were now built to compete with the railways in place of new railways being built to compete with the canals. The conditions had shifted. But all was in vain. Already at an early period the rivalry of the canals had been overcome;[2] by 1872 the influence of the

art. 61, in Picard, Chemins de fer français, t. iv, p. 71. As to the difficulties to which even this has given rise, see Aucoc, Droit administratif, t. iii, pp. 779 *et seq*.

[1] *Cf.* sec. 3.

[2] In 1865, of the four thousand miles of water and river communication in England and Scotland, about one-third had been amalgamated with the railways. Royal Commission (1867), Rep. App. qu. 9899 *et seq*.

canals as competing factors was infinitesimal.[1] The railways were the victors; competition had again failed.

On the continent the condition is the same. Everywhere the canals have been losing their traffic. Even when owned by the state, their efficacy is a thing of the past, although in such cases there can naturally be no consolidation with the private railways.[2] Isolated efforts are yet made to further the construction of new canals, but the better opinion now recognizes the ultimate uselessness of such attempts.

Although the movement has not progressed quite so far in the United States, the tendency is the same. From 1830 to 1850 the canals were formidable competitors of the railways, but from that time on the private canals were gradually bought up, while the state canals were either abandoned, sold, or reduced to a state of utter decrepitude. The efforts of the Clinton league in New York were unable to arrest the movement. In 1886 an expert witness stated to the Senate committee: "I do not think that there is a canal in the United States, except the Erie, that is not more or less controlled by the railroads."[3] The competition of artificial waterways can no longer be relied on.

In respect to natural waterways the matter is slightly different. The sea and navigable rivers cannot be subjected to a monopoly.[4] In such cases the competition is real and active, although only spasmodic in the case of internal navigation. The importance of the Erie canal, and the extent to which it really regulates the charges by rail, is due solely to the fact that

[1] Select Committee (1872), Rep., p. xxix. Also pp. xx-xxiv, with full references to the evidence. *Cf.* in general the admirable work of Freiherr von Weber, Die Wasserstrassen Nord-Europas (1881), S. 92-111. Also de Franqueville, Du régime des travaux publics en Angleterre, 2me éd. (1875), t. ii, pp. 274-306.

[2] *Cf.* Nördling, Die Wasserstrassenfrage in Frankreich, Preussen und Oesterreich (1885), esp. S. 28, 128, 158, 171-176. A French translation of this work has just been published.

[3] Cullom Committee Report, Test. (Wistar) 507. For a careful investigation of the whole question, *cf.* Mosler, Die Wasserstrassen in den Vereinigten Staaten (1877). Much valuable material may be found in Kupka, Die Verkehrsmittel in den Vereinigten Staaten (1883), S. 41-126.

[4] Yet in England there are instances even of this. *Cf.* Select Committee (1872), Rep., pp. xix, xx. Select Committee (1881), Evid. qu. 8133.

it is a link in the chain of natural waterways. But the influence of internal navigation is apt to be seriously exaggerated, and the exuberantly enthusiastic expressions of the Cullom report savor, it must be confessed, slightly of rhodomontade.[1]

Finally, it must not be overlooked that water competition, in so far as it is an important factor in internal transportation, is precisely the chief cause of local discriminations. Differential rates are due in great part, as we have seen, to the existence of competing centres. As long as the competition exists the discriminations must continue. Hence those who clamor for the construction of new waterways or the improvement of the old may indeed succeed in effecting a reduction of charges, but forget that they are only strengthening the causes of whose results they complain. To maintain competition and avoid discrimination is impossible.

The chief provisions of the federal law have now been discussed. There remains to be considered only the machinery to enforce the law, *i.e.*, the Interstate Commerce commission.

The commission idea is essentially a product of the Anglo-Saxon mind. On the continent of Europe direct administrative control has always been comparatively stringent, and the extent of state interference has been conditioned only by considerations of a political nature.[2] Almost every possible system has been tried; and if entire immunity from abuses has not been attained, it is not for lack of serious endeavors on the part of the govern-

---

[1] "The manifest destiny of our country points unerringly to this *emancipation of the waters* as its next great work, a fitting sequel to the emancipation of the slave, a a destiny not of war, but of beneficence and peace, to which the heart of the nation turns as spontaneously and resistlessly as the waters of its great river flow to the Gulf." Report, p. 175. *Cf.* with this "manifest destiny" the figures as to the decadence of the Erie canal in Statistics regarding the Movement of Eastbound and Westbound Traffic over the Trunk Lines, *etc.* (1885), pp. 16, 17; also Report on the Internal Commerce of the United States (1885), pp. 408–414. The Windom Committee likewise favored government canals. But the value of their suggestions may be inferred from the fact that they also recommended one or two government railways to regulate the private lines. Senate Select Committee on Transportation Routes to the Seaboard, Report (1874), pp. 187–242.

[2] Weber, Nationalität und Eisenbahnpolitik (1876). Audiganne, Les Chemins de fer d'aujourd'hui et dans cent ans (1858–1862).

ments. In no country was the public nature of the railway business lost sight of. Even where financial reasons led to the construction of railroads by private companies, the fostering and restraining action of the public authorities was never absent. The corporations were not able to dictate terms to the state.

In England the history was quite different. The railways, indeed, started out as humble suppliants for favors, but governmental action confined itself to seemingly guarded restrictions in the charters, such as maximum clauses and limitations of dividends, all of which were soon shown to be utterly powerless to prevent abuses. The railways increased so rapidly that their position soon became that of dictators, in place of suppliants. Warnings of able men like Morrison went unheeded.[1] Praiseworthy attempts were still made by far-sighted statesmen, but the railway opposition was sufficiently powerful to crush all interference. Lord Seymour's bill of 1840 provided for the appointment, by the Board of Trade, of railway inspectors, who should have the right to "remonstrate" with the companies.[2] But the law remained a dead letter, and in 1842 Gladstone brought in another bill giving the Board of Trade inspectors certain compulsory powers.[3] This law was not more successful than its predecessor, and finally, as the outcome of the great investigation of 1844, a commission was appointed within the Board of Trade and put in activity in 1845. It was known as Lord Dalhousie's Railway board, and was invested with extensive duties of examining all new projects. But although it worked hard, it discountenanced parallel roads and thus incurred the hostility of the railways and ultimately the jealousy of Parliament itself.[4] As a facetious member said, it attempted to do what five angels could not accomplish; and public opinion not coming to its rescue, it was abolished ingloriously the same year. Nothing daunted, however, the government brought in

---

[1] *Cf.* James Morrison, Speech in House of Commons, May 17, 1836; *id.*, The Influence of English Railway Legislation on Trade and Industry (1848), p. 86, and App., pp. 107, 158.

[2] 3 and 4 Vict. c. 97, An act for regulating railways.

[3] 5 and 6 Vict. c. 55, An act for the better regulation of railways, *etc.*

[4] *Cf.* Report on Railway Companies' Amalgamation (1872), p. vii.

a new bill constituting the Board of Railway Commissioners, in 1846, with moderately extensive powers.[1] But the railway interest again succeeded in robbing the bill of all its vitality, so that the only function left to the new commission was "inquiry and publicity." It vegetated for five years, accomplishing practically nothing, and was quietly abolished in 1851, while all its "extensive powers" were re-transferred to the Board of Trade.

For over twenty years the commission idea slumbered. Cardwell's act of 1854, the only serious attempt at governmental regulation during the interim, left the enforcement of its provisions to the common courts, and with the customary results. It was not until 1873 that the present railway commission was finally constituted. But although its activity has been incessant and the number of cases disposed of far greater than those previously adjudged by the purely legal tribunals, it has by no means achieved an unqualified success. The manifold complaints in the late investigation of 1881–82 and the proposals now pending to reconstitute and strengthen the commission bear ample testimony to this fact. The commission is practically a court for railway cases,[2] but its efficiency has been checked in three ways. Its jurisdiction is limited, its procedure is cumbrous and expensive, and its powers of enforcing judgment are restricted. Its jurisdiction is limited, with a few unimportant exceptions,[3] to cases arising under Cardwell's act of 1854, which forbids undue preferences and requires proper facilities. The commission has endeavored to widen its powers by interpretation, as, *e.g.*, in the case of transgression of the

---

[1] Accounts and Papers, 1846, vol. iii, p. 277; and the bill as passed May 21, in Accounts and Papers, 1847, vol. iii.

[2] Of the three members and two assistants, one must be a jurist. In questions of fact their decision is nominally final; if they think it a question of law, then they are to "state a case" in writing, and the matter goes up to the higher court, who are either to decide it, or to give their opinion as to the law and send the case back to the commission. But as the appellate court can issue a writ of *mandamus* compelling the commission to "state a case," the decisive power does not rest with the commissioners. *Cf.* Seventh Report Railway Commission, p. 3.

[3] Such as reasonableness of terminals, enforcement of through rates, agreements with canals, *etc.* 36 and 37 Vict. c. 48, §§ 8–11, 14–17. For list of cases decided up to 1882, *cf.* Select Committee (1881), Rep., App. no. 17, pp. 68–79.

charter maxima, but in this it has ignominiously failed.[1] Hence it cannot dispose of all complaints. Secondly, the procedure is unsatisfactory. The power of the railways is so great that the private shippers refrain from complaints for fear of reprisals. The weapons of retaliation in the hands of the companies have been ruthlessly employed.[2] But even if the shipper determines to brave the opposition of the railway, the expense is so enormous as to induce him in many cases to let the litigation drop.[3] The usefulness of the commission is thus greatly impaired. Finally, the means of enforcing judgment are sadly insufficient. The decisions of the commission refer only to the future, not to the past. Its "injunction" does not enable the complainant to recover damages. Furthermore, the companies sometimes flatly refuse to obey the decisions until finally ratified by the appellate courts, and even then they frequently contrive to evade the judgment.[4] The English corporations are far less amenable to the force of public opinion than the American. In short, although arbitrary personal discriminations are comparatively

---

[1] Brown *vs.* Great Western, Eighth Report Railway Commission, p. 4; App., 74–77. The high court of judicature issued a writ of prohibition against the commission. Select Committee on Railways (1882), p. 201. In Scotland it was different. Fifth Report, p. 8.

[2] "A man must be very chary in bringing an action against a railway company." Select Committee (1881), Evid. qu. 3745. A colliery company complained of overcharges, and the railway refused to transport the coal at all. Evid. (1881), pp. 138–142. A similar case arose with an iron company, and when the railway was compelled to take the goods, it sent them at such inconvenient times and added so many other vexations that the iron company was compelled to compromise. *Ibid.*, pp. 200, 237, 238. A firm in Bedford complained of exorbitant terminals, and the railway retaliated by raising the rates to Bedford more than one hundred per cent, and not to other parts of the line. *Ibid.*, p. 26. A brick and tile manufacturer complained of the rates, and the railway compelled him to prepay the charges, which were immediately raised fifty per cent. Evid. (1882), p. 220.

[3] A local board spent in one case £2500, and then abandoned the contest for lack of funds. Evid. (1881), p. 447.

[4] In a case against the Great North of Scotland the railway company was defeated after a stubborn fight, but reduced its rates only to the particular station in question and continued to make illegal charges to all the other stations. A separate suit would have been necessary in each case. Evid. (1881), p. 207. In the Neston case the overcharges were continued notwithstanding a decision by the appellate court. "There is no power to enforce obedience to the law." Evid. (1881), qu. 3094, and pp. 140 *et seq.*

rare,[1] owing to the greater development of combination, it may well be doubted whether the railway commission has produced a state of affairs much, if at all, better than that which existed prior to its inception. The new bill of 1887 emphasizes the feeling of necessity for a much more thoroughgoing reform.

In the United States the commission idea has two independent sources — the Granger movement and the public sentiment of Massachusetts. The policy of the American commonwealths has gone through three phases: the period of state aid and partial regulation, to 1845 or 1850; the period of *laissez faire*, to 1870; the period of active governmental interference, to the present. The moderate state regulation of the first period was due to the supposed analogy between railways and canals or highways. This varied naturally with the different sections of the country — from the railways owned and managed by the state, as in Georgia and Pennsylvania, to the charter regulations of charges in New York, and the limitations of dividends in New England. When the rates were fixed, they were based on the canal and turnpike tolls. The immoderate state aid to railways, again, was due to the mania for internal improvements during the thirties and forties. The scanty legislation of this period remained in great part unenforced because of the desire and necessity of more extended means of communication, and thus the commonwealth gradually ushered in the second phase of the development, that of *laissez faire* and unlimited competition. The system of special charters was succeeded by that of general railroad laws which exacted only a few formalities.[2] Not only were the railways left to themselves, but the belief in the absolute efficacy of unalloyed competition was so strong as to lead to a logical carrying out of the theory. No parallel or competing companies were authorized to consolidate.[3]

---

[1] But they still occur. *Cf.* Evidence (1881), qu. 1730–1737, where one shipper was compelled to abandon business. As to allowance for quantity, see qu. 11,804 *et seq.*

[2] So in New York the law of 1848, and finally that of 1850, which permits any twenty-five persons to form a company and file its articles when $1000 per mile is subscribed and $100 actually paid in. So in Illinois in 1849, and in the other states in the following decade.

[3] The railways of course avoided these provisions through the instrumentality of leases for long periods.

The more lines, the more competition; the more competition, the more benefits to the public — that was the theory.

The results of this policy soon became apparent. The crisis of 1857 brought disaster on the country; but other causes, like the wild-cat banks, were at work, besides the railways. Then came the war, which silenced all discussion for a time. But with the close of the war and the advent of wild railway construction in 1867, coupled with the prodigious development of the agricultural interests, the fruits of this unlimited freedom were seen. A system of the most reckless swindling and the most outrageous discriminations arose, such as has never existed before or since in any civilized society. The corporations regarded themselves as purely private money-making enterprises, and seemed not to have the faintest conception of any duties to the public. In the West the abuses were further intensified by the fact of absentee ownership,[1] so that the situation became intolerable. In response to repeated demands for redress, the railways flatly denied the right of the state to interfere with them at all. Things went from bad to worse.

It was as a protest against this attitude that the Granger movement arose. The National Grange, established in 1867 purely as a means of mutual improvement and protection for the farmers,[2] was soon drawn into the political warfare against the railroads. At first moderate in their demands, they now became extravagantly violent in word and action.[3] But while the Grangers demanded strict regulation they still believed in the saving force of competition. Failing to see that the bad results of which they complained were due to prohibition of combination, they made the prohibition still stronger. They allowed free competition between the roads, and then hoped to

---

[1] "The whole story is told in these two words — absentee ownership. While the Western patron was plundered, the Eastern proprietor was robbed." Report of Illinois Railroad Commission (1874), p. 17.

[2] *Cf.* Report of New Jersey Bureau of Statistics of Labor (1886), part vi; and Cloud, Monopolies and the People (1873).

[3] At the general convention at Springfield, 1873, it was resolved that the railways "have proved themselves of as arbitrary extortion and opposed to free institutions as the feudal barons of the Middle Ages." Other favorite phrases were "money-sharks" and "bloated bondholders."

legislate away the results of free competition. Competition was still the panacea. That the railroads did not act justly was their fault; *ergo*, said the Grangers, enforce free competition and prevent by legislation the perversion of the principle. That is, they attacked the problem in just the wrong way; they permitted the cause to remain, and hoped to remove the results; and in this they necessarily failed.

The hot-bed of the movement was in Illinois, where the constitution of 1870 adopted provisions of a stringent nature. The law of 1871 forbade any discriminations at all, and after its unconstitutionality had been proved, was followed by the law of 1873 which gave the commissioners power to fix rates. Iowa, Minnesota, Michigan, Ohio, Wisconsin, followed with maximum, *pro rata*, and short-haul laws, often fixing the rates or giving the commissions absolute and mandatory powers.[1] But the crudity of the laws was shown by the haste with which they were repealed.[2] The political results of the Granger movement indeed were of inestimable importance in putting an end to the arrogant pretensions of the corporations and in producing the sweeping decisions which finally settled the power of the states to regulate its creatures.[3] But the legal question was one thing; the economic question was another. The Granger movement was economically as unwise as it was politically important and successful. The compulsory commissions were an avowed failure.

Far better results were achieved by the advisory or supervisory commissions, of which Massachusetts afforded the first and most successful example. As Charles Francis Adams himself declares, it hit upon the correct method of legislative control by what was at the time nothing but a "happy guess."[4]

---

[1] For these various laws (Iowa 1874, Minn. 1871, Mich. 1871, Ohio 1873, Wis. 1874), see Cullom Rep., pp. 71–74, 98–102, 109–111, 119, 135–137.

[2] Minn. 1875, Wis. 1876, Iowa 1878. In Michigan and Ohio the laws were not enforced. In Illinois the powers of the commission were not used after the decision of the Granger cases. *Cf.* my preceding article, POLITICAL SCIENCE QUARTERLY, June, 1887, pp. 245, 259; or this essay, pp. 23, 27.

[3] Mun *vs.* Illinois, *etc.*, 4 Otto, 113–187. Decided in 1876.

[4] Cullom Committee Rep., Test. p. 1202. *Cf.* State Railroad Commissions, published by *The Railroad Gazette*, 1883.

Instituted in 1869 without extensive powers, it gradually concentrated the force of public opinion upon each particular abuse, and by its admirable reports, lucid explanations, and impartial decisions succeeded in producing a hitherto unheard-of harmony between the railways and the public.[1] Massachusetts still remains the chief type of advisory commissions. Many other states, and notably New York and Iowa, possess commissions of this nature, and the commissioners themselves object to any undue extension of their powers.[2] Their lack of authority and the support of a vigorous public sentiment have been the secret of their success. Even the Illinois commission, which possesses the authority to fix rates, has voluntarily adopted the Massachusetts principle of arbitration as more efficacious,[3] and the Kansas commission has made use of its discretionary power to place a very liberal interpretation on some rather stringent laws.[4] The chief instances of compulsory commissions to-day are to be found in the South. The Georgia commission promulgates from time to time a standard tariff, but it uses the authority with such wide discretion as to preserve the interests of the railways.[5] The Alabama commission possesses what is virtually the French power of *homologation*. New Hampshire is the only northern state with a compulsory commission; but the complaints were so few that the rates actually in force were accepted as the standard rates.[6]

The Interstate Commerce commission is thus in accord with the better experience of the American commonwealths, in that

---

[1] By ch. 338 of laws of 1885, the board was given powers to fix rates in a particular case; but it was a case of interstate commerce, and thus beyond their purview.

[2] As to New York, *cf.* Report of Railroad Com. (1884), p. 65; (1885), p. xxxiv *et seq.* As to Iowa, see Report Com. (1884), p. 43; (1885), p. 56. As to Illinois, see Report Com. (1884), Moore *vs.* Ill. Central.

[3] *Cf.* Report of its chief commissioner in Cullom Test., 734.

[4] Report Kansas Com. 1883, p. 28.

[5] Eleventh Rep. Ga. Com. (1885), p. 12; Twelfth, Thirteenth, and Fourteenth Reports (1886), p. 5.

[6] The compulsory commissions to-day are: Ga., S.C., Ala., Tenn., Miss., Cal., N.H. The advisory commissions are: Mass., N.Y., Ia., Wis., Minn., Mich., Col., Dak., Neb., Va. In Kan., Ill., Mo., and Ky., the powers are somewhat broader, but not rigidly exercised. In Conn., Me., Vt., R.I., O., the duties are mainly those of inspection.

it is invested with only moderate powers. It may investigate any matter falling within the purview of the act, whether the complaint be made by private individual, railway, or state commission, or it may institute inquiries on its own motion without any complaint whatever. If its recommendations are not accepted by the common carrier, the circuit court, and ultimately the supreme court, is to give the final decision, the report of the commission being *prima facie* evidence of the facts. The commission thus has only discretionary, not absolute, powers; and its success will depend largely upon the character of its decisions and the possibility of concentrating public sentiment on the question at issue. Whether it will attempt, like the English commission of 1845, to do "what five angels could not accomplish," is perhaps not an entirely settled point. But it is safe to say that not even five demigods could satisfactorily adjust all the complaints arising on 150,000 miles of railroad.

Our conclusions may now be summarized. The federal law contains provisions of undoubted value. Among these the enforced publicity of tariffs and projected uniformity of accounts deserve the heartiest commendation. Nothing is more conducive to strict impartiality toward the shippers and to perfect integrity toward the owners than the consciousness of public accountability. Secrecy has ever been the father of duplicity and favoritism. No one indeed can be legislated into righteousness, but the noonday glare of open responsibility is the strongest possible preventive of gross injustice. All those sections, therefore, which demand publication of the tariffs, submission of agreements, and eventual uniformity of accounts, must be acknowledged eminently wise provisions. In like manner the institution of a commission with moderate powers to serve as a medium of this responsibility and as an interpreter of the public demands must be unqualifiedly commended. Mere legislation is impotent without a proper machinery to enforce the decrees, and reliance on the judicial branch of the government has always been found inadequate.

Of more doubtful value, however, are the clauses which

attempt to ensure equitable charges. The definition of unjust discrimination is necessarily so vague as to be susceptible of varied interpretations. In itself it settles nothing. In so far as preferential rates are concerned, the law is guilty of a grave mistake in prohibiting pools. The crying evil of railway management to-day is personal discrimination. No mere legislative penalties will successfully abolish this. Pools are perhaps not a completely satisfactory solution of the problem; although as adjuncts to our traffic associations, they have accomplished incalculable good. They must rather be regarded as a temporary palliative, as a step in the onward march to final consolidation. But their prohibition at the present time is premature and unwise, and unnecessarily jeopardizes the success of the law. The underlying principle of pools — that of checking undue competition and ensuring uniformity of rates — will undoubtedly reappear in another form, most probably in agreements to give adequate "differentials." But these new agreements will be still more deficient in stability and coercive power than were the pools, and the ultimate outcome promises to be a more complete combination, a more thoroughgoing frustration of the competition which the law seeks to establish. Competition is the handmaid of personal discrimination.

Finally, the curtailment of local discriminations through the short-haul clause is a double-edged sword. It is intended to benefit the public, but if strictly enforced it would in many cases injure the public. As a check to arbitrary management and the systematic disregard of less favored localities, it is indeed defensible. But the important factors of water and foreign competition and long distance traffic must not be overlooked. As long as these exist, local discriminations will be absolutely necessary. The mere claim that existing business relations have been built up through the medium of differential rates and that their abolition would throw all trade into confusion, is not a sufficiently valid reason to oppose the law. For if these differential rates are unjust, even temporary distress cannot be pleaded as an excuse for continued injustice. But it has been shown that certain local discriminations are not unjust.

Value of service as a subordinate principle justifies carefully guarded infractions of the short-haul clause. Without these infractions we would soon attain the double result of ruining the railways in favor of their water competitors and of voluntarily abdicating the advanced position which improved means of transportation have given us. Each section of the country would be separated from the rest by the strongest of mutually protective tariffs. Either the commission must frequently relax the rule, or it must so liberally construe the clause as to permit wide local discriminations in specific cases. The latter policy has fortunately been already initiated by the opinion in the Louisville and Nashville case. Otherwise it would have needed but little foresight to predict grave inconvenience to the public and a speedy repeal of the law.

The Interstate Commerce act thus contains some serious blunders in the midst of many wise provisions. But on the whole, it is a cheering sign of the determination to grapple with evident evils. To conclude that it will at once remove the chief abuses would be far too optimistic. The condition of affairs will in most respects remain very much as it was. Personal discriminations at this moment are little, if at all, less frequent than before the passage of the law, and they will not be stopped by legislative authority. The main hope for the future lies in the further elaboration of the railway federations or traffic associations, to which most of the advance thus far made is ascribable, and whose complete history, never yet told, I must reserve for another time and place. Their importance, both past and present, has been phenomenally neglected. But the value of the Interstate Commerce law lies in the fact that it for the first time in our history subjects the railways to national supervision, and that it is designed to enforce a publicity and responsibility which are the prerequisites to all healthy reform. The federal law is a tentative step, but a step in the right direction. It embodies the expression of a principle which is destined to remain and which is capable of a fruitful development. On this account it deserves a hearty welcome.

www.ingramcontent.com/pod-product-compliance
Lightning Source LLC
Chambersburg PA
CBHW032246080426
42735CB00008B/1022